Office 2007: New Features

Student Manual

Office 2007: New Features

Series Product Managers:	Charles G. Blum and Adam A. Wilcox
Writer:	Steve English
Developmental Editor:	Laurie Perry
Copyeditor:	Ken Maher
Keytester:	Cliff Coryea
Series Designer:	Adam A. Wilcox

COPYRIGHT © 2007 Axzo Press

ALL RIGHTS RESERVED. No part of this work may be reproduced, transcribed, or used in any form or by any means—graphic, electronic, or mechanical, including photocopying, recording, taping, Web distribution, or information storage and retrieval systems—without the prior written permission of the publisher.

For more information, go to www.axzopress.com.

Trademarks

ILT Series is a trademark of Axzo Press.

Some of the product names and company names used in this book have been used for identification purposes only and may be trademarks or registered trademarks of their respective manufacturers and sellers.

Disclaimer

We reserve the right to revise this publication and make changes from time to time in its content without notice.

Student Manual
ISBN 10: 1-4239-5119-0
ISBN 13: 978-1-4239-5119-3

Student Manual with data CD
ISBN 10: 1-4239-5121-2
ISBN 13: 978-1-4239-5121-6

Printed in the United States of America

1 2 3 4 5 GL 10 09 08

Contents

Introduction   iii
Topic A: About the manual...iv
Topic B: Setting your expectations..vii
Topic C: Re-keying the course xi

The Office 2007 interface   1-1
Topic A: The Office Button menu 1-2
Topic B: The Ribbon 1-8
Topic C: The Mini toolbar 1-22
Topic D: The Quick Access toolbar and the Status bar 1-26
Unit summary: The Office 2007 interface 1-32

The Office XML file format   2-1
Topic A: The Office XML format 2-2
Topic B: Office XML format compatibility 2-4
Unit summary: The Office XML file format..................................2-11

New Word features   3-1
Topic A: Formatting 3-2
Topic B: Quick Parts and Building Blocks...................................3-10
Topic C: Shared documents...3-17
Unit summary: New Word features..3-23

New Excel features   4-1
Topic A: Larger worksheet size..4-2
Topic B: Charts and reports..4-3
Topic C: Table options 4-14
Topic D: PivotTables 4-24
Topic E: Excel Services...4-28
Unit summary: New Excel features..4-29

New PowerPoint features   5-1
Topic A: Dynamic SmartArt graphics 5-2
Topic B: Slide libraries..5-6
Topic C: Sharing presentations..5-7
Topic D: Custom layouts 5-12
Unit summary: New PowerPoint features 5-16

New Outlook features   6-1
Topic A: Content management tools 6-2
Topic B: The To-Do Bar..6-13
Topic C: Shared content 6-17
Unit summary: New Outlook features...6-30

New Access features   7-1
Topic A: Data features 7-2
Topic B: Reports..7-19
Unit summary: New Access features 7-27

Course summary   S-1

    Topic A: Course summary S-2

    Topic B: Continued learning after class S-4

Quick reference   Q-1

Glossary   G-1

Index   I-1

Introduction

After reading this introduction, you'll know how to:

A Use ILT Series training manuals in general.

B Use prerequisites, a target student description, course objectives, and a skills inventory to set your expectations properly for the course.

C Re-key this course after class.

Topic A: About the manual

ILT Series philosophy

ILT Series training manuals facilitate your learning by providing structured interaction with the software itself. While we provide text to explain difficult concepts, the hands-on activities are the focus of our courses. By paying close attention as your instructor leads you through these activities, you'll learn the skills and concepts effectively.

We believe strongly in the instructor-led class. During class, focus on your instructor. Our manuals are designed and written to facilitate your interaction with your instructor, and not to call attention to themselves.

We believe in the basic approach of setting expectations, delivering instruction, and providing summary and review afterwards. For this reason, lessons begin with objectives and end with summaries. We also provide overall course objectives and a course summary to provide both an introduction to and closure on the entire course.

Manual components

The manuals contain these major components:

- Table of contents
- Introduction
- Units
- Course summary
- Quick reference
- Glossary
- Index

Each element is described below.

Table of contents

The table of contents acts as a learning roadmap.

Introduction

The introduction contains information about our training philosophy and our manual components, features, and conventions. It contains target student, prerequisite, objective, and setup information for the specific course.

Units

Units are the largest structural component of the course content. A unit begins with a title page that lists objectives for each major subdivision, or topic, within the unit. Within each topic, conceptual and explanatory information alternates with hands-on activities. Units conclude with a summary comprising one paragraph for each topic, and an independent practice activity that gives you an opportunity to practice the skills you've learned.

The conceptual information takes the form of text paragraphs, exhibits, lists, and tables. The activities are structured in two columns, one telling you what to do, the other providing explanations, descriptions, and graphics.

Course summary

This section provides a text summary of the entire course. It's useful for providing closure at the end of the course. The course summary also indicates the next course in this series, if there is one, and lists additional resources you might find useful as you continue to learn about the software.

Quick reference

The quick reference is an at-a-glance job aid summarizing some of the more common features of the software.

Glossary

The glossary provides definitions for all of the key terms used in this course.

Index

The index at the end of this manual makes it easy for you to find information about a particular software component, feature, or concept.

Manual conventions

We've tried to keep the number of elements and the types of formatting to a minimum in the manuals. This aids in clarity and makes the manuals more elegant looking. But there are some conventions and icons you should know about.

Item	Description
Italic text	In conceptual text, indicates a new term or feature.
Bold text	In unit summaries, indicates a key term or concept. In an independent practice activity, indicates an explicit item that you select, choose, or type.
`Code font`	Indicates code or syntax.
`Longer strings of ▶ code will look ▶ like this.`	In the hands-on activities, any code that's too long to fit on a single line is divided into segments by one or more continuation characters (▶). This code should be entered as a continuous string of text.
Select **bold item**	In the left column of hands-on activities, bold sans-serif text indicates an explicit item that you select, choose, or type.
Keycaps like (↵ ENTER)	Indicate a key on the keyboard you must press.

Hands-on activities

The hands-on activities are the most important parts of our manuals. They're divided into two primary columns. The "Here's how" column gives short instructions to you about what to do. The "Here's why" column provides explanations, graphics, and clarifications. Here's a sample:

Do it!

A-1: Creating a commission formula

Here's how	Here's why
1 Open Sales	This is an oversimplified sales compensation worksheet. It shows sales totals, commissions, and incentives for five sales reps.
2 Observe the contents of cell F4	F4 ▼ = =E4*C_Rate The commission rate formulas use the name "C_Rate" instead of a value for the commission rate.

For these activities, we've provided a collection of data files designed to help you learn each skill in a real-world business context. As you work through the activities, you modify and update these files. Of course, you might make a mistake and therefore want to re-key the activity starting from scratch. To make it easy to start over, you rename each data file at the end of the first activity in which the file is modified. Our convention for renaming files is to add the word "My" to the beginning of the file name. In the above activity, for example, a file called "Sales" is being used for the first time. At the end of this activity, you save the file as "My sales," thus leaving the "Sales" file unchanged. If you make a mistake, you can start over using the original "Sales" file.

In some activities, however, it might not be practical to rename the data file. If you want to retry one of these activities, ask your instructor for a fresh copy of the original data file.

Topic B: Setting your expectations

Properly setting your expectations is essential to your success. This topic will help you do that by providing:

- Prerequisites for this course
- A description of the target student
- A list of the objectives for the course
- A skills assessment for the course

Course prerequisites

Before taking this course, you should be familiar with personal computers and the use of a keyboard and a mouse. Furthermore, this course assumes that you've completed the following courses or have equivalent experience:

- *Windows XP: Basic*
- Basic-level courses for all Office 2003 programs, including Word, PowerPoint, Excel, Outlook, and Access.

Target student

Before taking this course, you should have some experience using the applications in a previous version of Microsoft Office—preferably Microsoft Office 2003. You'll get the most out of this course if your goal is to become familiar with new features introduced in Word, Excel, PowerPoint, Outlook, and Access for Office 2007.

Course objectives

These overall course objectives will give you an idea about what to expect from the course. It's also possible that they'll help you see that this course isn't the right one for you. If you think you either lack the prerequisite knowledge or already know most of the subject matter to be covered, you should let your instructor know that you think you are misplaced in the class.

After completing this course, you'll know how to:

- Use the Office 2007 user interface, including the Microsoft Office Button, Ribbon tabs and Ribbon groups, galleries, contextual Ribbon tabs, Live Preview, the Dialog Box Launcher, the Document Information Panel, the Mini toolbar, and the Quick Access toolbar.

- Discuss the benefits of the XML file format, save files to older Office formats, use macro and non-macro file formats, and discuss file converters available for older versions of Office applications.

- Use Word features including styles, themes, and Quick Parts; compare two versions of a document, and save Word files to a static format, such as XPS or PDF.

- Use new Excel features including charts and reports, table options, structured referencing, and PivotTables.

- Use new PowerPoint features, including SmartArt graphics, slide libraries, presentation sharing features, and slide formatting.

- Use new Outlook features, including Instant Search, Color Categories, attachment previews, RSS feeds, the To-Do Bar, Internet calendars, calendar snapshots, and electronic business cards.

- Use new Access features, such as tabbed windows, lookup fields, attachment data types, e-mail data collection, Layout view, and sorting, filtering, and grouping report data.

Skills inventory

Use the following form to gauge your skill level entering the class. For each skill listed, rate your familiarity from 1 to 5, with five being the most familiar. *This isn't a test.* Rather, it's intended to provide you with an idea of where you're starting from at the beginning of class. If you're wholly unfamiliar with all the skills, you might not be ready for the class. If you think you already understand all of the skills, you might need to move on to the next course in the series. In either case, you should let your instructor know as soon as possible.

Skill	1	2	3	4	5
Using the Microsoft Office Button menu					
Using Ribbon tabs and Ribbon groups					
Using contextual Ribbon tabs					
Using galleries					
Using Live Preview					
Opening a dialog box by using the Dialog Box Launcher					
Adding information to the Document Information Panel					
Formatting content with the Mini toolbar					
Using and customizing the Quick Access toolbar					
Discussing the XML file format					
Saving files to older Office formats					
Using macro and non-macro file formats					
Using styles					
Using themes					
Using Quick Parts					
Comparing two versions of a document					
Saving files as static documents					
Creating charts					
Creating reports in Excel					
Creating and formatting tables in Excel					
Writing formulas that use structured referencing					
Creating and formatting PivotTables					

Office 2007: New Features

Skill	1	2	3	4	5
Converting bulleted lists to SmartArt in PowerPoint					
Creating slide libraries					
Creating custom slide layouts					
Using Instant Search to locate content in Outlook					
Organizing content using Color Categories					
Previewing an e-mail attachment					
Using RSS feeds					
Using the To-Do Bar					
E-mailing calendar snapshots					
Creating and sharing customized electronic business cards					
Using the Lookup field in Access					
Attaching files to an Access field					
Collecting Access data by using e-mail					
Creating reports in Access					

Introduction **xi**

Topic C: Re-keying the course

If you have the proper hardware and software, you can re-key this course after class. This section explains what you need in order to do so and how to do it.

The Windows operating system and the Microsoft Office 2007 suite are subject to continual updating by Microsoft. The versions of each that you install are by definition different from the versions that we used to prepare this course. The setup process described here may vary slightly from what you will encounter. This also applies to activities and screen shots throughout the course.

Hardware requirements

To re-key this course, your personal computer must have:

- A keyboard and a mouse
- Pentium 550 MHz processor (or higher)
- 256 MB RAM (or higher)
- 4 GB available hard disk space
- CD-ROM drive
- SVGA at 1024 × 768, or higher resolution monitor

Software requirements

You'll need the following software:

- Windows XP, Windows Vista, or Windows Server 2003
- Microsoft Office 2007
- The Microsoft Save as PDF or XPS Add-in for 2007 Microsoft Office programs. (If this isn't installed, you can't complete activity C-3 in the unit, "New Word features," and activity C-1 in the unit, "New PowerPoint features.")
- If you're using Windows XP, install the Microsoft XPS Essentials Pack. (If this isn't installed, can't complete activity C-3 in the unit, "New Word features.") If you're using Windows Vista, this software isn't required.

Network requirements

The following network components and connectivity are also required for this course:

- Internet access, for the following purposes:
  - Updating the Windows operating system and Microsoft Office 2007 at update.microsoft.com
  - Downloading the Student Data files (if necessary)
  - Downloading the Microsoft Save as PDF or XPS Add-in for 2007 Microsoft Office programs from www.microsoft.com/downloads.
  - Downloading the Microsoft XPS Essentials Pack from www.microsoft.com/downloads
- A valid e-mail address for Outlook configuration. (You need to send and receive e-mail throughout the unit, "New Outlook features.")

Setup instructions to re-key the course

Because this course requires an Exchange server and Outlook mail clients, it would be impossible to duplicate the classroom setup on your own. If you have Outlook 2007 mail capabilities, you can re-key the activities. However, keep in mind that the contents of your Inbox and other Outlook folders will differ from those shown in this manual.

Before you re-key the course, you need to perform the following steps.

1   Open Internet Explorer and navigate to update.microsoft.com. Update the operating system with the latest critical updates and service packs.

2   If you don't have the data CD that came with this manual, download the Student Data files for the course. You can download the data directly to your computer.

   a   Connect to www.courseilt.com/instructor_tools.html.

   b   Click the link for Microsoft Office 2007 to display a page of course listings, and then click the link for Office 2007: New Features.

   c   Click the link for downloading the Student Data files, and follow the instructions that appear on your screen.

3   Create a student data folder and copy the Student Data files to that folder.

CertBlaster software

CertBlaster pre- and post-assessment software is available for this course. To download and install this free software, complete the following steps:

1   Go to www.courseilt.com/certblaster.

2   Click the link for Office 2007.

3   Save the .EXE file to a folder on your hard drive. (Note: If you skip this step, the CertBlaster software will not install correctly.)

4   Click Start and choose Run.

5   Click Browse and then navigate to the folder that contains the .EXE file.

6   Select the .EXE file and click Open.

7   Click OK and follow the on-screen instructions. When prompted for the password, enter **c_2007**.

Unit 1

The Office 2007 interface

Unit time: 75 minutes

Complete this unit, and you'll know how to:

A Use the new Office Button menu and customize the application options.

B Use the Ribbon components, Live Preview, the Dialog Box Launcher, and the Document Information Panel.

C Format document elements using the Mini toolbar and shortcut menus.

D Use and customize the Quick Access toolbar, and use the Status bar.

Topic A: The Office Button menu

Explanation

For Office 2007, Microsoft completely redesigned the user interface that supports commands in Office applications. The most noticeable change is that the File menu has been replaced by the Office Button.

Office Button

Exhibit 1-1: The Office Button

When clicked, the Office Button displays the familiar File menu commands, as well as a list of the nine most recently opened files, as shown in Exhibit 1-2. You can open a file you were working on in your last session simply by clicking the Office Button and then clicking the file name in the Recent Documents list.

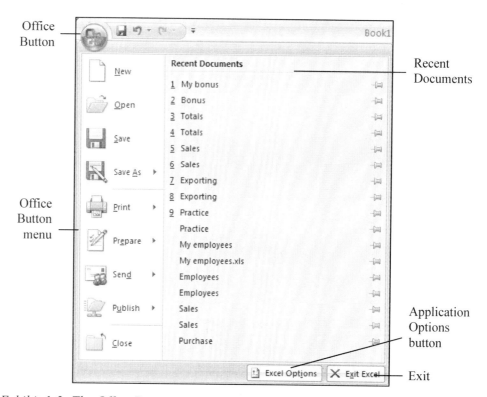

Exhibit 1-2: The Office Button menu in Excel

The Office Button menu contains commands for opening, saving, closing, and managing Office files. There are minor variations among Access, Excel, PowerPoint, and Word, but in general, the Office Button in any of these applications includes the items in the following table.

Item	Description
New	Opens the New dialog box. From here you can begin a blank file or begin a file from a template.
Open	Opens the Open dialog box. From here, you can navigate to a file and open it.
Save	Saves the current file.
Save As	Saves the current file under another name, in a different file format, as shown in Exhibit 1-3, or publishes the file as a static document, such as a PDF or XPS file.
Print	Prints the file or launches Print Preview.
Prepare	(Not in Access.) Enters file properties, inspects the file for private information, restricts permission to specific users, adds a digital signature, or marks as final.
Send	(Not in Access.) E-mails a copy of the file or sends a copy by Internet fax.
Publish	Saves the file to a document management server, creates a document workspace using Office SharePoint Server 2007, or displays other publishing options.
Close	Closes the current file. If changes were made, you're prompted to save it.
Manage	(Access only.) Compacts and repairs the database file, backs up the database file, displays database properties, or launches the Linked Table Manager.
E-mail	(Access only.) Packages the database as CAB and assigns a digital signature.
Application Options	Opens the Options dialog box for the application, where you can set application defaults and customize the application for your use.
Exit application	Closes the application. If changes were made to the currently open file, you will be prompted to save it before exiting.

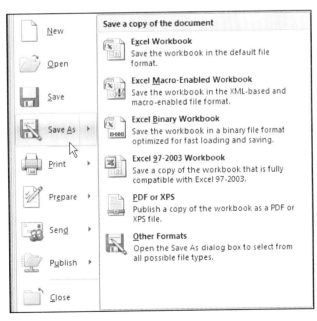

Exhibit 1-3: The Save As submenu

1–4 Office 2007: New Features

Do it!

A-1: Viewing Office Button commands

Here's how	Here's why
1 Click **Start** and choose **All Programs**, **Microsoft Office**, **Microsoft Office Excel 2007**	To start Excel 2007. A blank worksheet appears.
2 Click	To display the Office Button menu.
Choose **New**	To open the New Workbook dialog box. You can double-click the Blank Workbook or click Create to create a new document.
Click **Cancel**	To close the dialog box.
3 Click the Office Button	To display the menu.
Observe the Recent Documents list	This list displays the last 17 files opened in this application. You can pin any or all of these files to the list.
Point to **Open**	This option opens the Open dialog box. You can navigate to the desired folder and open a file.
Point to **Save**	This option saves the current file.
4 Point to **Save As**	While the arrow indicates additional options, you don't need to point directly at the arrow to see the save as options. All Microsoft Office 2007 applications provide options for saving a file in the Office 97-2003 format, and other formats, as shown in Exhibit 1-3.
5 Point to **Print**	To see the options for printing or previewing the file.
6 Point to **Prepare**	To see the options for defining properties and finalizing the file, so that it can be published or shared with others. You'll explore finalizing a document later.
7 Point to **Send**	To see the options for sending a copy of the file as an e-mail attachment or as an Internet fax.
8 Point to **Publish**	To see the options for sharing your file using a document management server or creating a document workspace.
9 Point to **Close**	This option closes the active file.

The Office 2007 interface **1–5**

Application settings

Explanation

An application's *Options dialog box* contains default settings for how the application starts and operates. For example, you might want to change the format in which data appears on screen, or change the number of worksheets that are created when you open a new workbook. You can use the application's Options dialog box, as shown in Exhibit 1-4, to change these and other defaults.

To open an application's Options dialog box, click the Office Button and click the application Options button. Each application includes settings divided into categories that are specific to its needs and operation. From the left side of the dialog box, click a category to view its settings. The following categories are common to most of the Office applications:

Category	Description
Popular	Setting application defaults.
Formulas	Configuring formulas, performance, and error processing.
Proofing	Configuring the spellchecker and other correction features.
Save	Configuring backup and autosave functions.
Advanced	Setting advanced application defaults.
Customize	Adding frequently used commands to the Quick Access Toolbar, as well as commands that don't occur on one of the standard Ribbon tabs.
Add-ins	Managing plug-ins and other extensions that might be developed for the application.
Trust Center	Configuring privacy and computer security-related options.
Resources	Upgrading and repairing Microsoft Office.

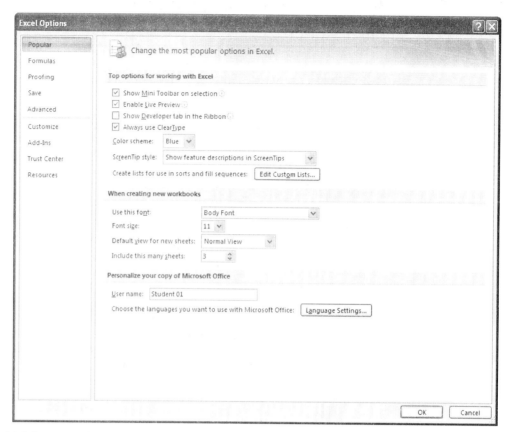

Exhibit 1-4: The Excel Options dialog box

The Office 2007 interface   **1–7**

Do it!   **A-2:   Changing the application options**

Here's how	Here's why
1 From the Office Button menu, click **Excel Options**	(The Excel Options button is located in the lower-right corner.) To open the Excel Options dialog box.
Observe the categories	Located on the left side of the dialog box. You can click these to display various settings. Many of the settings will look familiar.
2 Verify that Popular is selected	To display the Popular category settings. This category includes options for setting application defaults.
Under Personalize your copy of Office, in the User name box, enter your name	Personalize your copy of Office User name: Student01
Under Top options for working with Excel, click **Edit Custom Lists**	To open the Custom Lists dialog box. You'll create a custom list that can be used in Outlander Spices workbooks.
3 In the List entries box, enter **North, South, East, Central, West**	List entries: North, South, East, Central, West
	Many of Outlander Spices' sales worksheets are broken down by sales regions. A predefined list of regions can be useful when creating new worksheets.
Click **Add**	Custom lists: NEW LIST Sun, Mon, Tue, Wed, Thu, Fri, S Sunday, Monday, Tuesday, Wee Jan, Feb, Mar, Apr, May, Jun, J January, February, March, April North, South, East, Central, We
	The list of sales regions joins the other sequences in the Custom Lists dialog box.
Click **OK**	To close the Custom Lists dialog box and return to the Excel Options dialog box.
4 Click **OK**	To close the Excel Options dialog box.

Topic B: The Ribbon

Explanation

The original interface of menus and toolbars created for previous Office versions grew to include over a thousand commands. The new Ribbon interface makes it faster and easier for users to find the commands they need and can support additional growth in Office applications.

The Ribbon tabs and groups

In each Office application, the Ribbon is divided into tabs, as shown in Exhibit 1-5. The *tabs* display the commands and menus that apply to a specific set of actions, such as Home, Insert, and Page Layout. Each tab is divided into *groups*, such as Clipboard, Font, Alignment, and so on. Within each group are commands, buttons, and menus. The size of the buttons adjusts to accommodate the size of the open window.

Exhibit 1-5: The Ribbon in Excel

Galleries

Many menus have been replaced with galleries. Instead of displaying a menu of things to do, a *gallery* typically displays a graphical representation of the results of a command, as shown in Exhibit 1-6.

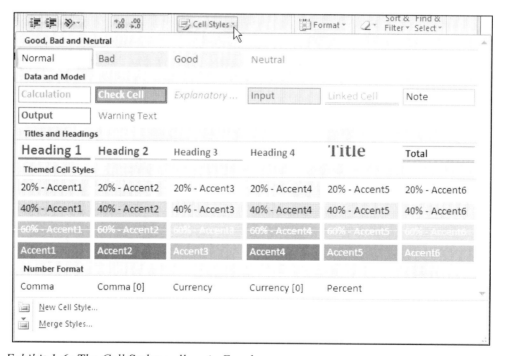

Exhibit 1-6: The Cell Styles gallery in Excel

The Office 2007 interface 1–9

Commands, lists and menus

On the Ribbon, you find commands, lists, galleries, and menus, as shown in Exhibit 1-7. The type of control that displays in a group depends on the nature of the task that it performs.

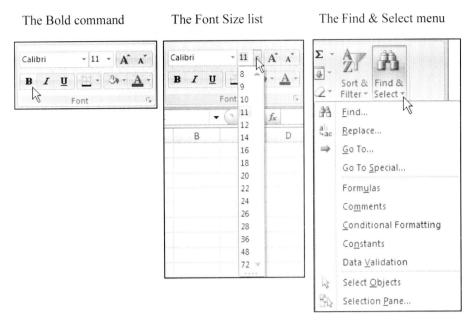

Exhibit 1-7: A command, list, and menu from Excel

1–10 Office 2007: New Features

Do it!

B-1: Using the Ribbon

Here's how	Here's why
1 Observe the Ribbon	As shown in Exhibit 1-5, the Ribbon is divided into multiple tabs. Other Office applications might use more or fewer tabs. In Excel, the Home tab displays by default.
2 Observe the Home tab	The Home tab is divided into groups, each of which contains commands and menus.
3 Activate the Insert tab	This tab displays objects that you might want to insert into an Excel worksheet.
Activate the other Ribbon tabs	To view their contents.
Activate the Home tab again	
4 In the Styles group, point to **Conditional Formatting**	A Super Tooltip describes conditional formatting.
5 In the Font group, click the arrow on the right side of the **Font** list	A list of fonts displays.
Click anywhere on the worksheet	To close the Font list.
6 In the Styles group, click **Cell Styles**	To display a gallery of cell styles, as shown in Exhibit 1-6.
Click anywhere on the worksheet	To close the Cell Styles gallery.
7 In the Editing group, click **Find & Select**	To display a menu of commands, as shown in Exhibit 1-7.
Close the Find & Select menu	

Contextual Ribbon tabs

Explanation

Some Ribbon tabs remain hidden until needed. *Contextual Ribbon tabs* display only if the object that they control is inserted or selected.

For example, the Design, Layout, and Format tabs display in Excel when you insert or select a chart, as shown in Exhibit 1-8.

Exhibit 1-8: The Design, Layout, and Format tabs in Excel

Do it!

B-2: Using contextual Ribbon tabs

Here's how	Here's why
1 Click [Office Button]	To display its menu.
Choose **Open**	
Navigate to the current unit folder and open Bonus	You'll open an Excel workbook and insert objects that trigger contextual Ribbon tabs.
2 From the Office Button menu, choose **Save As**	To open the Save As dialog box.
Save the file as **My bonus**	
3 Select A3:E7	You'll insert a chart for the quarter sales.
4 Activate the Insert tab	
5 In the Charts group, click **Bar**	To display the gallery of bar charts.
Click as shown	
	To insert a clustered 3-D bar chart in the worksheet.
6 Observe the Ribbon	Three Chart Tools tabs appear. The Design tab is activated by default, as shown in Exhibit 1-8.
7 Activate the Layout tab	The Layout tab includes menus and commands to change the appearance of the selected chart.

1–12 Office 2007: New Features

8	Activate the Format tab	The Format tab includes menus and commands for reformatting the selected chart.
9	Click anywhere in the worksheet	(To deselect the chart.) The Chart Tools are no longer displayed.
	Drag the chart down and to the right	(To expose the cells hidden behind it.) When you click the chart, the Chart Tools groups appear again.
10	Select A1	You'll insert a picture and observe the changes to the Ribbon.
	Activate the Insert tab	
	In the Illustrations group, click **Picture**	

		The Insert Picture dialog box opens.
	Insert **Logo**	Navigate to the current unit folder, select Logo, and click Insert.
11	Observe the Ribbon	The Picture Tools Format tab appears and is activated, because the picture is selected.
	Observe the groups	They include Adjust, Picture Styles, Arrange, and Size.
12	Select the chart	The Chart Tools tabs appear on the Ribbon.
	Activate the Format tab	The groups, and the menus and commands in them, are different for charts from what they are for pictures.
	Update the workbook	Click the Office Button and choose Save.

The Office 2007 interface   **1-13**

Live Preview

Explanation Live Preview is a feature of some lists and menus in Office applications. When you point to a selection in a list or gallery that features Live Preview, the selected text or object in the document displays the effect of that selection, as illustrated in Exhibit 1-9.

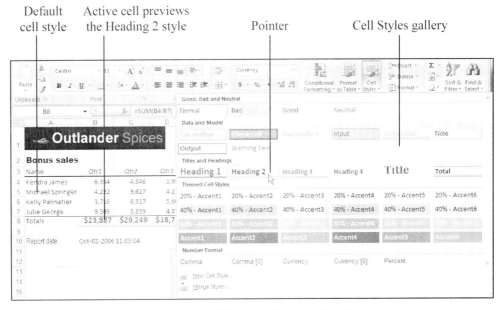

Exhibit 1-9: Live Preview for the Cell Styles gallery in Excel

1–14   Office 2007: New Features

Do it!

B-3:   Using Live Preview

Here's how	Here's why
1 Select A2	You'll use Live Preview to view fonts for the text in this cell.
2 Verify that the Home tab is activated	
In the Font group, click the arrow beside the Font list	To display the font list.
3 Point to **Bodoni MT Poster Compressed**	In the font list.
Observe the text in A2	The text is previewed in Bodoni MT Compressed.
Point to other fonts in the list	The text in A2 shows a preview of each font.
Choose **Arial Black**	To format the text in A2.
4 Format A10 as **Arial Narrow**	Select A10, then click the arrow beside the Font list, and select Arial Narrow.
5 Select B8:E8	You'll use Live Preview to view styles for these cells.
In the Styles group, click **Cell Styles**	To display the Cell Styles gallery, as shown in Exhibit 1-9.
Point to several different Cell Styles in the gallery	The styles are previewed in B8:E8.
6 Under Themed Cell Styles, click as shown	

Themed Cell Styles

20% - Accent1	20% - Accent2
40% - Accent1	40% - Accent2
60% - Accent1	60% - Accent2
Accent1	Accent2

To choose 40% - Accent 2 as the cell style for the range.

7 Update the workbook	

Dialog Box Launcher

Explanation

In most Office applications, there are more commands and settings than can be displayed on the Ribbon. Dialog boxes are available, where necessary, to display more detailed settings. To open a dialog box, click the *Dialog Box Launcher* that appears in the lower-right corner of many groups on the Ribbon, as shown in Exhibit 1-10.

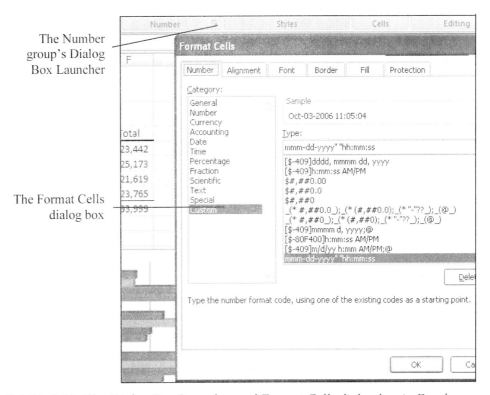

Exhibit 1-10: The Dialog Box Launcher and Format Cells dialog box in Excel

1–16 Office 2007: New Features

Do it!

B-4: Using the Dialog Box Launcher

Here's how	Here's why
1 Select B10	You'll format the date in this cell.
2 In the Number group, click the arrow beside the Number Format list, as indicated	
	To display frequently used formats.
Observe the date formats that are available in this list	They include Short Date and Long Date, two commonly used date formats. You'll use a different format.
Click anywhere in the worksheet	To close the list.
3 In the Number group, click [icon]	(The Dialog Box Launcher icon is in the lower-right corner.) The Format Cells dialog box opens with the Number tab activated, as shown in Exhibit 1-10.
In the Category list, select **Date**	
	To display a list of date formats.
Under Type, select **March 14, 2001**	
	(Scroll down to see the format.) To select this date format.
Click **OK**	To close the Format Cells dialog box and apply this format.
4 Update the workbook	

Document Information Panel

Explanation

You can attach metadata to Office files using the *Document Information Panel*. *Metadata tags* describe and define the properties of the file. Metadata tags include:

- Author
- Title
- Subject
- Keywords
- Category
- Status
- Comments

These tags can display when you point to a file in Windows Explorer, as shown in Exhibit 1-11. To display the Document Information Panel, click the Office Button to display its menu. Then choose Prepare, Properties. The Document Information Panel appears below the Ribbon, as shown in Exhibit 1-12.

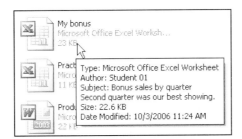

Exhibit 1-11: Metadata tags displayed in Windows Explorer

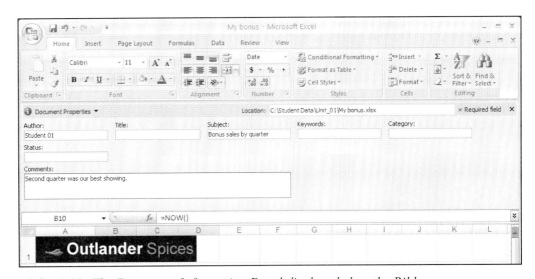

Exhibit 1-12: The Document Information Panel displays below the Ribbon

1–18 Office 2007: New Features

Do it!

B-5: Using the Document Information Panel

Here's how	Here's why
1 Click	To display the Office Button menu. You'll enter information in the Document Information Panel.
Choose **Prepare**, **Properties**	The Document Information Panel displays below the Ribbon.
2 In the Author box, enter your name	To identify yourself as the author of this file.
3 In the Subject box, enter **Bonus sales by quarter**	To describe the worksheet.
4 In the Comments box, enter **Second quarter was our best showing.**	
5 Click the Close box in the Document Information Panel	* = Required field ⊠ Close the Document Information Panel
	Click the X in the top-right corner of the Document Information Panel.
6 Update and close the workbook	
7 Open Windows Explorer	Right-click Start and choose Explore.
Navigate to the current unit folder in C:\Student Data and point to My bonus	As shown in Exhibit 1-11, a Tooltip displays the Author, Subject, and Comments information that you entered in the Document Information Panel for this file.
Close Windows Explorer	

The Office 2007 interface   **1–19**

Finishing a file

Explanation

Excel, PowerPoint, and Word include an option in the Office Button menu to *finish* a file. This option is intended for files that you've finished editing and are ready to share with a larger audience. There are minor variations between applications, but finishing a file includes the following:

Item	Description
Properties	Insert titles, descriptions, keywords, and other metadata in the file.
Inspect Document	Inspect the file, including any metadata, for hidden content or personal data that shouldn't be included in a shared file.
Encrypt Document	Add encryption to protect the file from unauthorized access.
Add a Digital Signature	If you've created a digital signature, you can add it to a file to verify that you are the author.
Mark as Final	Make the file read-only, so that no further changes can be made to it.
Run Compatibility Checker	Check the file for Office 2007 features that aren't supported by older versions of the application and will be lost if the file is saved in that format.

Do it!

B-6:   Finishing a document

Here's how	Here's why
1 Open My bonus	Click the Office Button and choose Open. Navigate to the current unit folder, select My bonus and click Open.
2 From the Office Button menu, choose **Prepare**, **Inspect Document**	The Document Inspector displays a list of content to be inspected. By default, all content options are checked. You're prompted to save your document before proceeding with the inspection.
Click **Yes**	To save the document.
3 Click **Inspect**	The Document Inspector displays content that might potentially compromise your security, confidentiality, or identity.
Observe the inspection results	You have the option to remove the content that might pose a problem.
Click **Close**	To close the Document Inspector without removing any potentially insecure content.

4 From the Office Button menu, choose **Prepare**, **Add a Digital Signature**	You'll add a digital signature so that users who read this document know that you were the last person to make changes to it. The Signature dialog box opens.
Click **OK**	The Get a Digital ID box appears.
5 Select **Create your own digital ID**	You can create a digital ID for local use, or get one from an external source that users on other computers can verify. For this activity, you'll create your own digital ID.
Click **OK**	(This might take a few moments.) A dialog box appears asking for your signature information.
Click **Create**	To accept the information as listed.
6 Click **Sign**	To sign the document. The Signature Confirmation box appears.
Click **OK**	The Signatures pane appears to the right of the worksheet.
7 Select any empty cell	You'll view the effects of digitally signing the document.
Type in the cell	This cell and all cells in the worksheet are locked.
Observe the title bar and the Ribbon	The title bar displays "Read-Only" and, on the Ribbon, most of the commands and menus on the tabs are disabled. To continue working with this file, you'll remove the signature for now.

8 In the Signatures pane, right-click the signature and choose **Remove Signature**	Student 01 10/3/20 ▼
	 👤 Sign Again...
	    Signature Details...
	    Signature Setup...
	    Remove Signature

	The Remove Signature dialog box appears.
Click **Yes**	To remove the digital signature. The Signature Removed dialog box appears.
Click **OK**	To close the dialog box.
Close the Signatures pane	Click the Close box in the pane.
9 Observe the Ribbon	The commands and menus are enabled again. Worksheet cells are no longer locked.

The Office 2007 interface   **1–21**

10	Click the Office Button and choose **Prepare**, **Run Compatibility Checker**	To open the Microsoft Office Excel – Compatibility Checker dialog box. You'll check this workbook for compatibility with earlier versions of Excel.
	Click **OK**	To close the dialog box.
11	From the Office Button menu, choose **Prepare**, **Mark as Final**	To mark this as the final copy of the workbook. The Microsoft Office Excel dialog box appears.
	Click **OK**	To save the workbook and mark it as the final copy.
	Click **OK** again	To close the message box explaining final documents.
12	Observe the title bar	My bonus.xlsx [Read-Only] - Microsoft Excel The workbook is designated read-only. Ribbon commands and menus are disabled, and the worksheet cells are locked.
	Observe the status bar	Ready The Marked as Final icon appears to the right of Ready.
13	Open the Document Information Panel	Click the Office Button and choose Prepare, Properties.
	Observe the Status box	Status: Final The document has been marked Final.
	Close the Document Information Panel	
14	From the Office Button menu, choose **Prepare**, **Mark as Final**	To unlock the workbook so that it can be edited again.
	Observe the title bar	The read-only designation is gone. The workbook can be edited again.
15	Close all open workbooks	Do not save changes, if prompted.
16	Close Excel	

Topic C: The Mini toolbar

Explanation

You can format text and numbers in Office applications without using the Ribbon. Right-clicking a selection displays the Mini toolbar and a shortcut menu.

The new Mini toolbar

The *Mini toolbar* is a set of commonly used formatting controls, such as Font, Color, or Alignment. As with other features, there are minor variations among applications. For example, as shown in Exhibit 1-13, the Excel Mini toolbar includes options to increase or decrease the number of decimal places in a number. These options don't display on the Mini toolbar in Word that's shown in Exhibit 1-14.

The *shortcut menu* displays below the Mini toolbar when you right-click a selection. It includes options that are specific to each Office application.

Exhibit 1-13: The Excel Mini toolbar

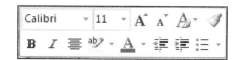

Exhibit 1-14: The Word Mini toolbar

Do it!

C-1: Using the Mini toolbar

Here's how	Here's why
1 Start Word 2007	(Click Start and choose All Programs, Microsoft Office, Microsoft Office Word 2007.) A blank document appears.
Open Product	From the current unit folder.
Save the file as **My product**	In the current unit folder.
2 In the document, select the spices from **Angelica Root** to **Turmeric**	To select the list of spices. If you point on or near the selected text, then the Mini toolbar appears.
Move the pointer slowly away from the Mini toolbar	The Mini toolbar fades. If you move too far from the Mini toolbar, it disappears. To make it reappear, you point to the selected text again.
Move the pointer back toward the Mini toolbar	The Mini toolbar becomes more distinct.
3 Click the arrow beside the Font list	To display the fonts.
Select **Times New Roman**	To change the font of the spices in the list.
4 Right-click the selected text	To display the shortcut menu. The Mini toolbar no longer fades away if you point away from it.
In the shortcut menu, click the arrow beside **Numbering**	To display the Numbering Library gallery.
Click as shown	To number the spices in the list.
5 Update the document	

Hide the Mini toolbar

Explanation

You can modify the application options so that the Mini toolbar isn't shown for selected text or objects. To do so, click the Office Button and click the application Options button.

In the Popular category settings, the most common options for working with the application are displayed at the top, as shown in Exhibit 1-15. Clear the Show Mini Toolbar on selection option to hide the Mini toolbar. Click OK to close the application Options dialog box.

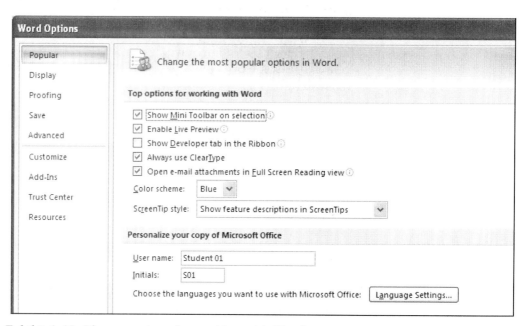

Exhibit 1-15: The top options for working with Word

The Office 2007 interface **1–25**

Do it!

C-2: Hiding the Mini toolbar

Here's how	Here's why
1 Open the Word Options dialog box	Click the Office Button and click Word Options.
2 In the left pane, verify that Popular is selected	To display the Popular category settings.
Under Top options for working with Word, clear **Show Mini Toolbar on selection**	Top options for working with Word ☐ Show Mini Toolbar on selection ⓘ ☑ Enable Live Preview ⓘ ☐ Show Developer tab in the Ribbon ⓘ
	To disable the Mini toolbar from appearing when you initially select text. However, it still appears when you right-click a selection.
Click **OK**	To close the dialog box.
3 Select **Angelica Root**	(At the top of the list.) Pointing to the selection doesn't launch the Mini toolbar automatically.
Right-click the selection	The Mini toolbar and the shortcut menu appear.
4 Restore the Mini toolbar to show on selection	Open the Word Options dialog box. In the left pane, select Popular (if necessary). Under Top options for working with Word, check Show Mini Toolbar on selection. Then click OK to close the dialog box.

1–26 Office 2007: New Features

Topic D: The Quick Access toolbar and the Status bar

Explanation

The *Quick Access toolbar* in Office applications is a convenient location for frequently used commands, including Save and Undo. The Status bar contains information about the current document, as well as controls for view switching, and zooming in and out.

Quick Access toolbar

By default the Quick Access toolbar is located beside the Office Button, above the Ribbon. You can change the position of the Quick Access toolbar so that it displays below the Ribbon. To do this, click the arrow on the right side and choose Show Below the Ribbon.

Do it!

D-1: Positioning the Quick Access toolbar

Here's how	Here's why
1 Click the arrow on the right side of the Quick Access toolbar	
Choose **Show Below the Ribbon**	The Quick Access toolbar moves from the top of the Word window frame to between the Ribbon and the formula bar.
2 Move the Quick Access toolbar back to its original position	Click the arrow and choose Show Above the Ribbon.

Adding a command to the Quick Access toolbar

Explanation

You can customize the Quick Access toolbar to include commands or other frequently used Ribbon elements, so that you don't have to navigate to those commands by using the Ribbon tabs or the Office Button. For example, if you work with a file that must be e-mailed to co-workers at the end of every session, you could place an e-mail command on the Quick Access toolbar.

You can add any elements from the Ribbon or the Office Button menu to the Quick Access toolbar, so that they're always visible. You can add groups, galleries, menus, lists, and commands. To add existing items to the Quick Access toolbar, right-click the Ribbon element and choose Add to Quick Access Toolbar. To add a dialog box, right-click the appropriate Dialog Box Launcher.

Microsoft has anticipated some commands that you might want to add. You can easily add these commands by clicking the arrow on the right side of the Quick Access toolbar, and selecting the desired command.

The Office 2007 interface **1–27**

Do it!

D-2: Adding a command to the Quick Access toolbar

Here's how	Here's why
1 Activate the View tab	You'll add a command to the Quick Access toolbar.
In the Window group, right-click **Switch Windows**	To display a shortcut menu for this button.
Choose **Add to Quick Access Toolbar**	Add to Quick Access Toolbar Customize Quick Access Toolbar... Show Quick Access Toolbar Below the Ribbon Minimize the Ribbon
Observe the Quick Access Toolbar	The Switch Windows button appears on the right side of the Quick Access toolbar, just before the dropdown arrow.
2 Open Employee	From the current unit folder.
3 Observe the Quick Access toolbar	The Switch Windows button remains available on the Quick Access toolbar for all documents.
4 Click the Switch Windows button	✓ 1 Employee 2 My product (On the Quick Access toolbar.) To display the list of open documents.
Choose **My product**	To switch to that document.

1–28 Office 2007: New Features

Adding hidden commands to the Quick Access toolbar

Explanation

You might want to use commands that don't appear anywhere in the default interface. To add a hidden command to the Quick Access toolbar, open the application Options dialog box and display the Customize category. In the list of commands, select an item, and click Add to add it to the Quick Access toolbar. Click OK.

To open the Word Options dialog box with the Customize settings displayed, do either of the following:

- From the Quick Access toolbar menu, choose More Commands.
- Right-click anywhere on the Ribbon, Office Button, or Quick Access toolbar, and choose Customize Quick Access Toolbar.

To add the commands:

1 From the Choose commands from list, select the commands that you want to see.

2 Select the desired command and click Add. The command appears in the Customize Quick Access Toolbar list.

3 Click OK.

Do it!

D-3: Using the Customize settings

Here's how	Here's why
1 Click 	To display the Office Button menu.
Click **Word Options**	To open the Word Options dialog box.
2 Select **Customize**	(In the list of categories on the left.) You can use this category to add frequently used commands to the Quick Access toolbar. This method is useful for adding commands that don't appear on any of the standard Ribbon tabs.
From Choose commands from, select **All Commands**	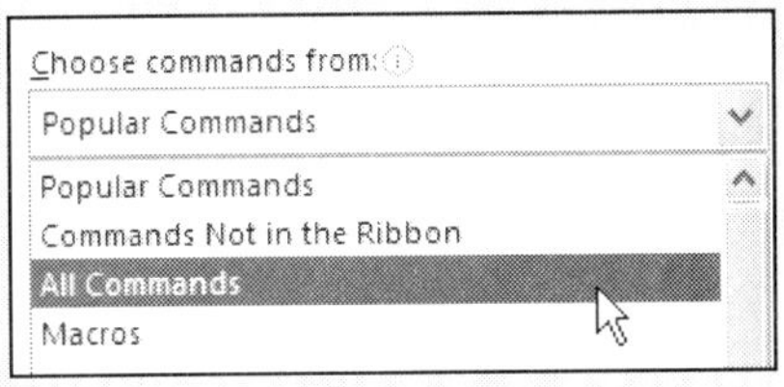Choose commands from: Popular Commands Popular Commands Commands Not in the Ribbon All Commands Macros
In the commands list, select **Close**	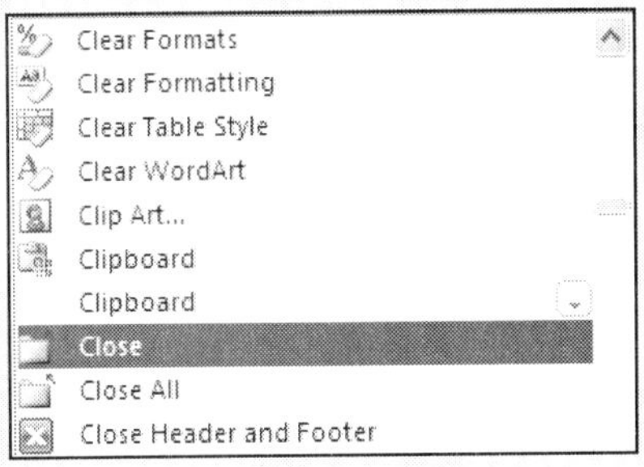Clear Formats Clear Formatting Clear Table Style Clear WordArt Clip Art... Clipboard Clipboard Close Close All Close Header and Footer Press the letter "C" to display quickly the commands that start with that letter.
Click **Add**	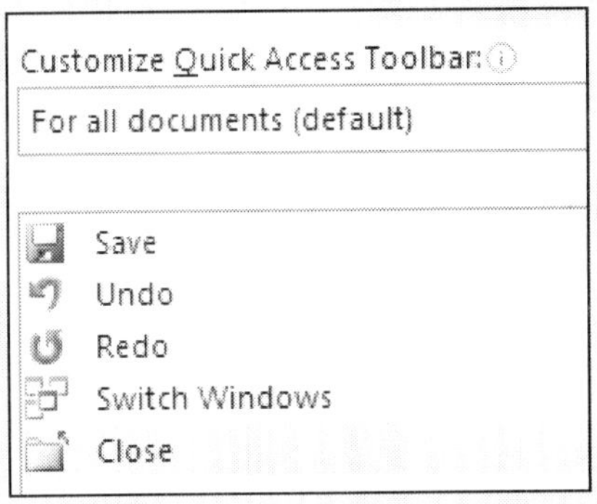Customize Quick Access Toolbar: For all documents (default) Save Undo Redo Switch Windows Close To add the Close command to the Quick Access toolbar for all documents.
3 Click **OK**	 To close the dialog box. The Close command now appears on the Quick Access toolbar.

The Status bar

Explanation

The Status bar at the bottom of the window frame displays information about the currently open file. For Access, Excel, PowerPoint, and Word, the Status bar also contains buttons to switch the view or window, as well as controls to zoom in and out.

The Status bar in Outlook displays the number of items in the current folder. For example, if the Inbox is active, the Status bar displays the number of messages in the Inbox.

View/Window switching

The right side of the status bar contains buttons to switch the view of the open file, as shown in Exhibit 1-16.

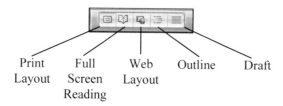

Exhibit 1-16: The Status bar buttons in Word

Zoom

The Status bar provides two ways to zoom in and out on a document, as shown in Exhibit 1-17. You can drag the slider bar to change the magnification. Or you can click the Zoom level button, and use the Zoom dialog box.

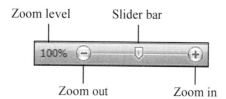

Exhibit 1-17: The Zoom buttons and slider bar

Do it!

D-4: Using the Status bar

Here's how	Here's why
1 Observe the right side of the Status bar	At the bottom of the window frame. The Print Layout button is active.
Point to each of the view buttons	A Tooltip displays each button's name.
Click [icon]	(The Web Layout button.) To view the document as it would appear if it were saved as a Web page and displayed in a browser.
2 Switch to Print Layout	Click the Print Layout button.
3 Drag the Zoom slider bar slightly to the left	[slider image: 71% − slider +]
	The zoom percentage on the Zoom button changes, and the view of the document page zooms out.
Click [+]	(The Zoom In button on the slider.) To zoom in to the nearest 10%.
Return the view to 100%	Keep clicking Zoom In until the Zoom level reads 100%.
4 Select **Caraway Seed**	In the list of spices on the page.
Zoom to approximately 300%	Drag the slider bar to the right. The selected text remains in the center of focus.
Return the view to 100%	Drag the slider bar or click Zoom Out.
5 Click Zoom level	[image: ≡ 100% −]
	To open the Zoom dialog box that's used to select a specific zoom percentage. If the document is in Print Layout view, you can choose to display the document at settings that are specific to the monitor, such as Whole page.
Click **Cancel**	To close the dialog box.
6 Close all open documents	You can use the Close button on the Quick Access toolbar.
Close Microsoft Word	

1-32   Office 2007: New Features

Unit summary: The Office 2007 interface

Topic A   In this topic, you explored the **Ribbon** elements, including tabs, groups, and galleries. Then, you used **Live Preview** to see formatting options in the document. Next, you opened dialog boxes by using the **Dialog Box Launcher**. Finally, you used the **Document Information Panel** to annotate a file.

Topic B   In this topic, you accessed the **Office Button menu**. Next, you changed the application settings by using the application **Options** button. Finally, you learned how to **finish** a document to prepare it to be shared with others.

Topic C   In this topic, you learned how to use the **Mini toolbar** and the shortcut menu to format items in a file.

Topic D   In this topic, you learned how to reposition and customize the **Quick Access toolbar**. Then, you learned how to use the **Status bar** to change the view of a document and zoom in and out.

Independent practice activity

In this activity, you'll format text using the shortcut menu. Then, you'll create a chart and change the design of that chart using a contextual tab. Next, you'll use Live Preview to help you choose a font for a cell. Then, you'll enter information in the Document Information Panel. Finally, you'll add a command to the Quick Access toolbar, and mark the workbook as final.

1 Start Excel 2007, if necessary.

2 Open Practice, and save the file as **My practice**.

3 Select A4:K5 and make the text bold. (*Hint*: Use the shortcut menu.)

4 Select A5:E6 and create a column chart. (*Hint*: Use the Insert tab.) Move the chart off of the worksheet data.

5 Change the chart style. (*Hint*: On the Design tab, use the Chart Styles group.)

6 Select A1. Use the Font list to preview several fonts, and choose one for the text in this cell.

7 Select B9:K9. Preview several cell styles, and choose one for these cells. (*Hint*: Click Cell Styles on the Home tab.)

8 Open the Document Information Panel. Enter your name as the author, and enter **District Sales** as the Subject. (*Hint*: Click the Office Button and choose Prepare, Properties.) Close the Document Information Panel.

9 Add the E-mail command to the Quick Access toolbar.

10 Save the workbook and mark it as final. Compare your workbook to the one shown in Exhibit 1-18.

11 Close the workbook and close Excel.

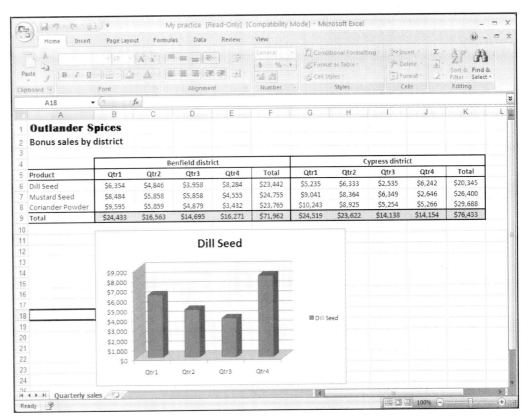

Exhibit 1-18: The workbook as it might appear after step 10

Review questions

1 What's the Office feature that's divided into tabs and groups and contains menus, commands, and lists?

  A Office Button

  B Ribbon

  C Quick Access toolbar

  D Status bar

2 What's the Office feature that resembles a list but displays a graphical representation of the result of an action?

  A Contextual tab

  B Ribbon list

  C Gallery

  D Office Button

3 Which type of tab is displayed only when the object it controls is inserted or selected?

   A Just-in-time tab

   B Standard tab

   C Ribbon tab

   D Contextual tab

4 How does Live Preview work?

5 What feature is used to enter metadata for a file, such as description, keywords, and other data?

   A File Properties dialog box

   B Document Information Panel

   C Document Properties pane

   D Status bar

6 How do you access the application Options dialog box?

   A Using the Office Button

   B Using the Customize tab

   C Choosing Tools, Options

   D Clicking Options in the Quick Access toolbar

7 What happens when you right-click selected text in Word?

   A The Font dialog box opens.

   B The Mini toolbar fades in and out.

   C The Mini toolbar and shortcut menu display.

   D The shortcut menu disappears.

8 You can add hidden commands to the Quick Access toolbar. True or false?

Unit 2

The Office XML file format

Unit time: 30 minutes

Complete this unit, and you'll know how to:

A Explain the benefits of the Office 2007 file format.

B Save files using the older Office formats, compare file sizes between Office 2007 format and older formats, use macro-enabled or macro-free file formats, and discuss file converters for previous versions of Office.

Topic A: The Office XML format

Explanation
Office 2007 uses a new, XML-based file format for Word, Excel, and PowerPoint files.

Benefits of XML file format

This file format offers a number of benefits, as described in the following table.

Benefit	Description
Size	Office 2007 files are typically smaller than their counterparts from earlier versions of Office, because Office 2007 applications compress their files.
Backward compatibility	The XML-based file format is now the default. However, Office 2007 applications can open files saved in previous versions, and can save files using the older binary file formats.
Data recovery	Files are saved in sections, then linked together when opened. If a section of a file is damaged or corrupted, the remainder of the file can often be opened and recovered.
Extensibility	The open XML format means that files can be addressed, read, and manipulated by any XML-compliant application. The file specifications are published and have a royalty-free license. Inserted data, such as images, are stored as separate file components and can be addressed and manipulated directly.
Privacy	Personal information, such as the author's name or comments, can be removed from the file by using the Document Inspector.
Macro detection	To avoid opening files with potentially dangerous macros, files containing VBA macros or ActiveX controls must be saved in a macro format that has a unique extension, such as .docm for Word documents and .xlsm for Excel workbooks.

Do it! **A-1:** **Discussing benefits of the Office XML format**

Questions and answers

1 What does the new file format mean in terms of file size?

2 How does the file format for Office 2007 differ from XML file formats released for earlier Office products?

3 Why is the new format considered more robust?

4 How can developers extend the functionality of Office 2007 files?

Topic B: Office XML format compatibility

Explanation

Office 2007 files can be saved to older Office formats, for users who still use previous versions of Office.

The 97-2003 format

To save the file in an older format, click the Office Button to display the menu. Point to the arrow beside Save As and choose the older format, as shown in Exhibit 2-1.

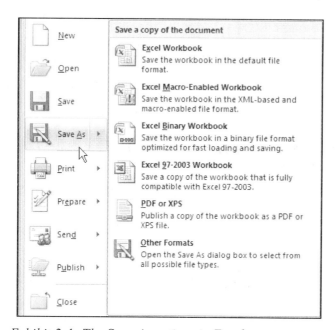

Exhibit 2-1: The Save As options in Excel

Compatibility Checker

Many Office applications include a Compatibility Checker function. This lists any features in an Office 2007 file that aren't compatible—and won't be available—when the file is saved to an earlier version. If you attempt to save an Office 2007 file to an older format, the Compatibility Checker prompts you if there are incompatible features in the file.

The Office XML file format **2–5**

Do it!

B-1: Saving files to older Office formats

Here's how	Here's why
1 Start Excel 2007	
Open Formatting	(From the current unit folder.) You'll save this workbook in the file format used by previous versions of Office.
2 Display the Office Button menu	Click the Office Button.
Point to **Save As**	
	To see the additional document formats, which include the Excel 97-2003 format, as shown in Exhibit 2-1.
3 Choose **Excel 97-2003 Workbook**	To open the Save As dialog box.
From the Save as type list, verify that Excel 97-2003 Workbook is displayed	File name: Formatting Save as type: Excel 97-2003 Workbook
Edit the File name box to read **My 2003 formatting**	
Click **Save**	The Compatibility Checker dialog box appears. A summary of the features not supported in this file type appears.
4 Observe the second item in the list	
	The first item describes an issue with conditional formatting. The second item describes an issue with a pivot table. The pivot table isn't critical to this workbook. You'll save in the older format without the pivot table.
Click **Continue**	To close the dialog box and finish saving the file. The pivot table is converted to ordinary text cells.
5 Close the workbook	

File sizes

Explanation

Office 2007 applications automatically compress their files when saving. When you open the file, the application extracts the file and displays it. The result is that, even though Office 2007's XML-based files are more feature-rich than those created in previous versions, they use less disk space.

Do it!

B-2: Comparing Office 2007 to Office 2003 file sizes

Here's how	Here's why
1 Display the Open dialog box	Click the Office Button and choose Open.
2 Point to **Formatting**	A Tooltip appears. The original version of the workbook has a file size of approximately 33 KB.
3 Point to **My 2003 formatting**	(This is the same file, saved in the older file format.) The file size that appears in the Tooltip is approximately 63 KB.
4 Click **Cancel**	To close the dialog box.

The Office XML file format **2–7**

Macro formats

Explanation

A macro is a very useful tool for automating repetitive tasks. However, macros can also be a security risk. Malicious software can be embedded in macros that execute unexpectedly.

Excel, PowerPoint, and Word can use two versions of the new XML-based file format. One version allows macros, the other doesn't. You can create files using the macro-free format that can then be shared in an organization with the knowledge that opening the file doesn't pose a security risk. The macro-free format is the default file format.

File formats

The table that follows lists file formats for Excel, PowerPoint, and Word.

Application	Macro-free	Macro-enabled
Excel	.xlsx	.xlsm
PowerPoint	.pptx	.pptm
Word	.docx	.docm

2–8 Office 2007: New Features

Do it!

B-3: Using macro formats

Here's how	Here's why
1 Open Macros	(From the current unit folder.) This workbook is identical to the Formatting data file, except that it contains a macro. You'll view the effect of file formats on macros.
2 A Security Warning might display, between the Ribbon and the formula bar	To alert you that macros have been disabled on your system.

> 🛡 **Security Warning** Macros have been disabled. | Options... |

Click **Options**	The Microsoft Office Security Options dialog box appears.
Select **Enable this content**	

More information

File Path: C:\Student Data\Unit_02\Macros.xlsm

○ Help protect me from unknown content (recommended)
◉ Enable this content

	To allow macros to run.
Click **OK**	To close the dialog box. The Security Warning disappears.
3 Select G5	You'll run the macro embedded in this file.
4 Press ⌜CTRL⌝ + ⌜M⌝	To launch the macro. The macro adds additional columns to the Bonus sales report, copying the month sequence and formatting in the title row and copying the sum formulas and formatting in the subtotal rows. The worksheet is now ready to accept additional sales data.

5 Save the workbook as an Excel Workbook with the name **My macros**	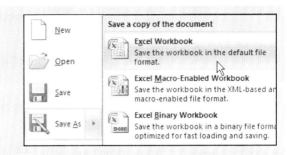
	In the Save As dialog box, verify that Excel Workbook (.xlsx) format appears in the Save as type list. The Microsoft Office Excel dialog box appears, to inform you that you've chosen a macro-free format.
Click **Yes**	To save the workbook in macro-free format.
Close the workbook	
6 Open My macros.xlsx	The workbook that you just saved in macro-free format.
Select K5	
Press CTRL + M	Nothing happens. Macros can't execute in a file saved in this format.
Close the workbook	
7 Close Excel	

2–10 Office 2007: New Features

Converters for previous releases

Explanation

Files created in Office 2007 applications can be opened in previous versions of Office if the author creates a copy in the older format. But if this isn't done, then users who have older versions of Office can't open the files.

Download the Compatibility Pack

Microsoft also offers a Microsoft Office Compatibility Pack that can be downloaded from Microsoft Online. This compatibility pack provides file converters for users of Office 2000, Office XP, and Office 2003. The converters, when installed, allow users with these older versions of Office to open Office 2007 files.

With the compatibility pack, you're able to open and edit the files. However, some objects that were created in Office 2007 might become static during the conversion process. Office 2007 templates can't be opened in previous Office releases, even with the compatibility pack.

Information Rights Management

Some Office 2007 files might be saved with Restricted Permission, using Information Rights Management (IRM). If these files are converted to older versions, any IRM restrictions are retained. Windows XP users need to have the Windows Rights Management Services (RMS) Client.

Do it!

B-4: Discussing converters for previous Office releases

Questions and answers
1 What do the XML file converters do?
2 For what previous versions of Office are converters available?
3 How do the converters interact with IRM?

The Office XML file format   **2–11**

Unit summary: The Office XML file format

Topic A   In this topic, you discussed benefits of the new **XML-based file format** as related to file size, backward compatibility, data recovery, and extensibility.

Topic B   In this topic, you saved Office 2007 files to **older file formats**. Then, you compared files saved in new and older versions of Office, and learned that Office 2007 files are smaller. Next, you saved files using **macro-free formats**. Finally, you learned about **file converters** available for previous versions of Office.

Independent practice activity

In this activity, you'll use Microsoft Word 2007 to save documents in the older Office format. Then you'll compare the file sizes of the two documents. Finally, you'll open a macro-enabled file and save it as a macro-free file.

1 Start Word 2007.

2 From the current unit folder, open Cookbook.

3 Save the document as **My 2003 cookbook** in Word 97-2003 Document format. (*Hint*: If the Compatibility Checker dialog box appears, click Continue to save the document without any new features that are incompatible with the previous format.)

4 Compare the file sizes of Cookbook.docx and My 2003 cookbook.doc.

5 Open Print.

6 Save the file as a macro-free document named **My print**.

7 Close all open documents, and close Word.

2–12 Office 2007: New Features

Review questions

1 How do Office 2007 file sizes compare to files saved in early versions of Office?

 A The file size is very similar.

 B Office 2007 files are always larger.

 C Office 2007 files are typically larger.

 D Office 2007 files are typically smaller.

2 Office 2007 files are considered more robust than earlier version files. True or false?

3 There's a security advantage of having the macro-free file format. True or false?

4 Which statement is true about using Office 2003 to open the new Office 2007 files?

 A Older versions of Office can't open Office 2007 files.

 B Older versions of Office can use converters to open Office 2007 files.

 C Files created with older versions of Office aren't compatible with Office 2007.

 D Only Office 2003 files can be opened in Office 2007.

5 Which extension is used for PowerPoint macro-enabled files?

 A docm

 B docx

 C pptx

 D pptm

3–1

Unit 3

New Word features

Unit time: 60 minutes

Complete this unit, and you'll know how to:

A Use styles to format content, format charts and shapes, and use themes to format documents.

B Use Quick Parts and Building Blocks, and add custom content.

C Discuss sharing documents in a workflow, compare two versions of a document, and save a document to a static format.

Topic A: Formatting

Explanation

Word 2007 makes it easy to format text with a style gallery. Formatting charts and other screen objects has also been enhanced by the new user interface. And using Themes makes it easy to format an entire document.

Styles

Styles are sets of formatting options that define the appearance of recurring text components, such as headings or body text. By using a style, you can apply several formatting options in one step, and you can ensure that all similar text components have identical formatting.

Word 2007 displays all styles in a gallery, as shown in Exhibit 3-1. The Styles gallery is located in the Styles group on the Home tab. Each style in the gallery shows a representation of the text style and a name for the style. You can use Live Preview to see the effect of a style on text by selecting the text, then pointing to a style in the gallery.

Word provides several predefined styles. For example, you can apply the Heading 1 style to format selected text as a heading. By default, when you create a new document, Word applies the Normal style to the entire document. You can create as many custom styles as needed.

Exhibit 3-1: The Styles gallery

New Word features   **3–3**

Do it!   **A-1:   Formatting content by using the Styles gallery**

Here's how	Here's why
1 Start Word 2007	If necessary.
Open Descriptions	(From the current unit folder.) You'll format the text using Styles.
Save the document as **My descriptions**	
2 Go to page 6	Press F5 and enter 6.
Select **Spice popularity**	At the top of the last page. You'll use Styles to apply formats.
3 Activate the Home tab	If necessary.
In the Styles group, click the More button, as indicated	AaBbCc AaBbCcl Heading 2 Heading 3 Change Styles ▾ Styles
	(The More button is on the right side of the Style list.) To display the Styles gallery.
Point to styles in the Styles gallery	Live Preview shows the effect of the style on the selected text.
4 Click **Title**	To apply this style to the text.
Deselect the text	Spice popularity

The popularity of any spice varies widely b illustrates this by displaying shipments of s quarter. |
| | To see that the new style has been applied. |
| 5 Update the document | |

Charts

Explanation

You can insert charts that are based on Excel worksheets into Word documents. The new user interface makes it easy to insert, format, and edit a chart.

To create a chart based on Excel data:

1 Activate the Insert tab.
2 In the Illustrations group, click Chart to open the Insert Chart dialog box, as shown in Exhibit 3-2.
3 In the category list on the left, choose a chart style.
4 In the pane on the right, choose a chart type.
5 Click OK to close the dialog box and insert the chart. A chart appears on the page, and an Excel workbook with sample data opens. The Design, Layout, and Format tabs display.
6 Edit the Excel workbook to use the data that you want to include in the chart. You can add, delete, or rename the column and row headings.
7 Use the Design, Layout, and Format tabs to customize the chart.

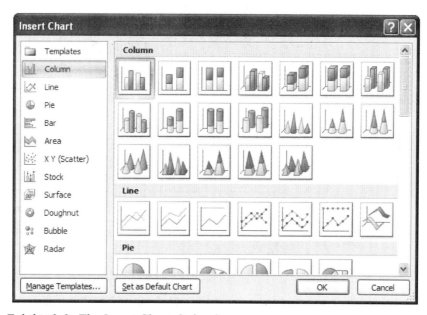

Exhibit 3-2: The Insert Chart dialog box

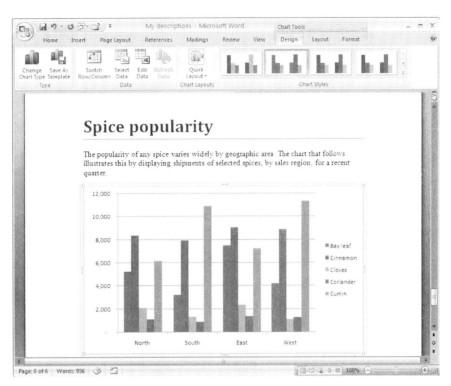

Exhibit 3-3: A chart added to a Word document

3–6 Office 2007: New Features

Do it!

A-2: Creating and formatting charts in Word

Here's how	Here's why
1 On the last page, place the insertion point below the text	(Use Ctrl+End to move there quickly.) You'll insert and format a chart.
Activate the Insert tab	
2 In the Illustrations group, click **Chart**	The Insert Chart dialog box opens, as shown in Exhibit 3-2.
In the category list on the left, select **Column**	(If necessary.) You'll add a column chart.
In the right pane, verify that Clustered Column is selected	To choose a type of column chart.
Click **OK**	An Excel window opens and displays a worksheet with sample data. The Word and Excel windows are arranged side by side.
3 Activate Word	A chart displays the sample data from the Excel worksheet. There are three data series and four categories in the chart.
4 Activate Excel	You'll change the data in the referenced Excel worksheet.
5 Select E1	You'll add a data series to the chart in Word by adding a column to the table in Excel.
Type **Series 4**	To give the new data series a name.
In E2:E5, enter **45**, **55**, **65**, and **75**, respectively	To add data to the new data series.
6 Maximize Word	Columns for the fourth data series have been added to the plot area of the chart, and the series name (Series 4) appears in the legend.
7 Maximize Excel	You'll replace the sample data with real data from an existing worksheet.

New Word features **3–7**

8	Open Shipments	From the current unit folder.
9	Select A4:F8	The quarterly spice shipments.
	Right-click and choose **Copy**	To copy this data.
10	Activate the Chart in Microsoft Office Word worksheet	Select the worksheet in the taskbar at the bottom of the window.

Select A1

	A	B	C	D	E
1		Series 1	Series 2	Series 3	Series 4
2	Category 1	4.3	2.4	2	45
3	Category 2	2.5	4.4	2	55
4	Category 3	3.5	1.8	3	65
5	Category 4	4.5	2.8	5	75
6					

	Right-click and choose **Paste**	The sample data is replaced with the data from the existing worksheet.
11	Activate My descriptions	The chart now displays the quarterly spice shipments, as shown in Exhibit 3-3.
	Update the document	
12	Close the Chart in Microsoft Office window	
	Close Shipments and close Excel	Word should be active.

Shapes

Explanation

You can edit and format other screen objects, such as shapes, by using galleries and Live Preview. To insert and format a shape object on a page:

1 Activate the Insert tab.

2 In the Illustrations group, click Shapes to display the Shapes gallery.

3 Select a shape, then drag to draw it on the page.

4 On the Format tab, use the galleries on this tab to select Shape Styles, colors, effects, and positioning. You can use Live Preview to see the effect of a selection just by pointing to it.

3–8 Office 2007: New Features

Do it!

A-3: Adding and formatting a shape

Here's how	Here's why
1 Activate the Insert tab	My descriptions should still be open. You'll add a diagram symbol to the page.
In the Illustrations group, click **Shapes**	
Under Basic Shapes, click **Rounded Rectangle**	
	The pointer changes to a plus sign.
2 Drag to create a rounded rectangle below the chart	The Drawing Tools Format tab is activated.
In the Shape Styles group, click the More button, as indicated	
	To display the Shape Styles gallery.
Point to any style	Live Preview shows the results on the page.
Point to several different styles in the gallery	To see the effect on the shape.
3 Click anywhere on the page	To close the Shape Styles gallery and keep the rectangle selected.
4 Click **Shadow Effects**	To open the Shadow Effects gallery.
Point to various shadow effects	To see them displayed on the object by Live Preview.
Close the gallery	Click anywhere on the page.
5 Use Live Preview to see 3-D effects	Click 3-D Options to open the menu. Then, click the arrow beside 3-D options to open the gallery. Point to selections in the gallery to see the results on the object. Then click the page to close the gallery.
6 Delete the rounded rectangle	Select the rectangle and press Delete.
7 Update and close the document	

Themes

Explanation

A *theme* is a named set of colors, fonts, and effects that's applied to all pages in a document to provide a consistent look to the document. When you apply a theme to a document, the formatting of the pages is changed, and the elements—such as background colors, heading styles, and table border colors—are customized based on the theme. After choosing a theme, the Font Color and Page Background Color galleries display colors from the theme. Each theme includes colors designed to complement one another.

To apply a theme, activate the Page Layout tab. In the Themes group, click Themes and select a theme to apply the theme's colors, fonts, and effects. If you want to apply only the colors, fonts, or effects for a particular theme, you can choose from the appropriate lists in the Themes group.

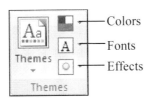

Exhibit 3-4: The Themes group on the Page Layout tab

Do it!

A-4: Applying themes

Here's how	Here's why
1 Open Themes	From the current unit folder.
Save the file as **My themes**	You'll use a theme to format this document.
2 Activate the Page Layout tab	
3 In the Themes group, click **Themes**	To display the Themes gallery.
Point to several themes in the gallery	Live Preview displays the results of the themes on the page.
Click **Opulent**	To apply the theme. The document heading text now displays a different font and color.
4 Update and close the file	

Topic B: Quick Parts and Building Blocks

Explanation

The *Quick Parts* menu provides a fast method of inserting properties, fields, page numbers in a Word document. In addition to these items, the Building Blocks Organizer contains a library of reusable document components, such as cover pages, headers and footers, and watermarks.

Quick Parts

You can insert properties, fields, or page numbers by using the Quick Parts menu, as shown in Exhibit 3-5.

Exhibit 3-5: The Quick Parts menu

Properties

You can choose Document Property in the Quick Parts menu to insert text in the document that's also included as metadata in the Document Information Panel. To add a title to both the document and the properties:

1. Activate the Insert tab.
2. In the Text group, choose Quick Parts, Document Property, Title. A tagged title field appears on the page.
3. Edit the title text to be added to the document.
4. Press Enter.
5. Point to the text. The Title tag appears.
6. Open the Document Information Panel. The text appears in the Title field.

Fields

To insert a field in a document:

1. Activate the Insert tab.
2. In the Text group, choose Quick Parts, Field. The Field dialog box appears.
3. Choose a field from the list. If necessary, choose properties and options to define that field.
4. Click OK to close the dialog box.

Do it!

B-1: Accessing Quick Parts

Here's how	Here's why
1 Open My descriptions	(From the current unit folder.) You'll view Quick Parts.
2 Activate the Insert tab	
In the Text group, click **Quick Parts**	The Quick Parts menu displays.
3 Point to **Document Property**	To see the Property submenu. This list includes fields that can be inserted into the document file, and that display in the Document Information Panel. They also display in a Tooltip when a user points to a file in Microsoft Explorer.
4 Select **Field...**	
	The Field dialog box opens, displaying a list of fields that can be inserted in a document.
Scroll through the Field names list	To view the selection of fields available.
Click **Cancel**	To close the Field dialog box.

Building Blocks Organizer

Explanation

Building blocks are commonly used document components, and the Building Block Organizer is a library containing these document components. To make the building blocks easier to find, they're divided into the following galleries, as shown in Exhibit 3-6:

- Autotext
- Cover Pages
- Equations
- Headers and Footers
- Page Numbers
- Tables
- Text Boxes
- Watermarks

Insert a Building Block in a document

To insert a Building Block:

1. Activate the Insert tab.
2. Choose Quick Parts, Building Blocks Organizer. The Building Blocks Organizer appears, as shown in Exhibit 3-6.
3. In the Building Blocks list, click the item that you want to insert into the document. The preview pane displays the item on your page and a short description of the selected building block.
4. Click Insert.
5. Click Close to close the Building Blocks Organizer.

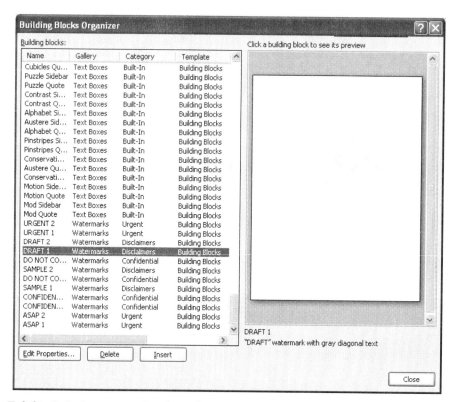

Exhibit 3-6: A watermark selected in the Building Blocks Organizer

Do it!

New Word features **3–13**

B-2: Using the Building Blocks Organizer

Here's how	Here's why
1 In My descriptions, verify that the insertion point is at the beginning of the document	You'll add a built-in Building Block to this document.
2 Activate the Insert tab	If necessary.
Click **Quick Parts** and select **Building Block Organizer...**	The Building Block Organizer dialog box displays. A listing of available building blocks appears on the left. When you click on any item in the list, it's previewed in the pane on the right.
3 Under Building blocks, click the Gallery column heading, as indicated	To sort the entries alphabetically by gallery.
4 Point to the divider between the Name and Gallery columns	The pointer changes to a double-sided arrow.
Drag to widen the Name column	To make the entries easier to read.
Scroll to the bottom of the list	To view the watermarks.
5 Click **DRAFT 1**	The preview pane displays a diagonal watermark on a page, as shown in Exhibit 3-6.
Click **Insert**	To insert the watermark and close the dialog box.
6 Scroll through the document	The watermark appears on every page.
7 Update and close the document	

Custom content

Explanation

You can add your own custom content to the Quick Parts gallery or to the Building Blocks Organizer. This can be a great timesaver if you've created document components that are reused often.

To add a Quick Part or Building Block:

1. Select the document component to be saved.
2. Activate the Insert tab.
3. Choose Quick Parts, Save Selection to Quick Part Gallery. The Create New Building Block dialog box appears, as shown in Exhibit 3-7.
4. Give the document component a name.
5. In the Gallery list, select Quick Parts to add the item directly to the Quick Parts gallery, or select a gallery in the Building Blocks Organizer.
6. Select or create a category, and enter a description.
7. Save the item in the default document template, or in the Building Blocks.dotx template.
8. Click OK to close the dialog box.

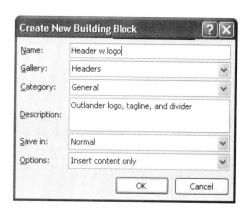

Exhibit 3-7: The Create New Building Block dialog box

New Word features **3–15**

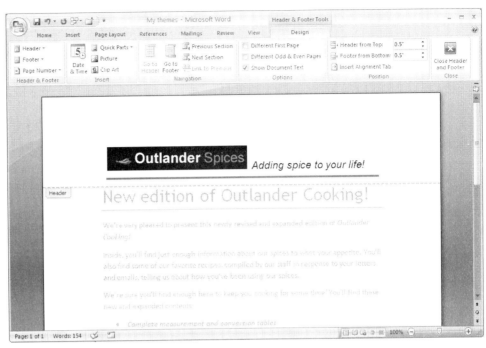

Exhibit 3-8: The new header with logo added to the document

Do it! **B-3: Adding custom Quick Parts**

Here's how	Here's why
1 Open HeaderBlock	(From the current unit folder.) You'll add a custom Building Block.
2 Observe the content at the top of the page	A text box includes a logo, some text, and a line.
3 Triple-click the text	To select the text and its text box.
4 On the Insert tab, click **Quick Parts**	
Select **Save Selection to Quick Part Gallery…**	The Create New Building Block dialog box appears.
5 Edit the Name box to read **Header w logo**	To create a meaningful name for this building block.
In the Gallery list, choose **Headers**	To sort this building block in the list of Headers.
In the Category list, choose **General**	(If necessary.) To enter this Building Block in a category.

3–16 Office 2007: New Features

6 In the Description box, enter **Outlander logo, tagline, and divider**	To describe this object for users.
In the Save In list, select **Normal**	(If necessary.) To save this Building Block in the default document template.
In the Options list, confirm that Insert Content Only is selected	Compare your dialog box to the one shown in Exhibit 3-7.
Click **OK**	To close the dialog box and add this object to the Building Blocks list in the Quick Parts menu.
7 Close the document	
8 Open My themes	You'll use Quick Parts to add this header to the document.
9 Place the insertion point to the left of the heading	
10 On the Insert tab, click **Quick Parts**, and select **Building Blocks Organizer...**	To open the Building Blocks Organizer dialog box.
Scroll down to the Headers entries in the Gallery column	
Click **Header w logo**	

Building blocks:

Name	Gallery	Category	Template
Conservative	Headers	Built-In	Building Blocks
Cubicles (Od...	Headers	Built-In	Building Blocks
Blank (Thre...	Headers	Built-In	Building Blocks
Header w logo	Headers	General	Normal
Blank	Headers	Built-In	Building Blocks
Contrast (O...	Headers	Built-In	Building Blocks

	To see the building block displayed in the preview pane.
Click **Insert**	To close the dialog box and insert the building block.
11 Observe the page	The Outlander logo, tag line, and divider display in the Header section at the top of the page, as shown in Exhibit 3-8.
12 Double-click anywhere on the page	To close the Header section. The logo is still visible but is grayed out, to indicate that it isn't editable while the Header section isn't active.
13 Update and close the document	
14 Close Word	

New Word features **3–17**

Topic C: Shared documents

Explanation

Producing a document is a collaborative effort in many organizations. For example, one member of a team might write the text, another might produce the graphics, and others might need to edit and approve the document before release.

Workflow

The path that a document follows before being finalized is called a *workflow*. A workflow might include many steps performed by many individuals. You can create automated workflows to manage a document's review cycle.

An author selects a predefined workflow from within Word. The workflow stores the document in a document library, where access to it can be restricted to specific users. When the document is ready for review or approval, the required team members automatically receive an e-mail informing them that the document is ready for them. When they've finished their tasks, they send the original author an e-mail that includes a workflow completion form that describes the document's status. The author can use document comparison tools in Word to compare the original document to the edited copy in the document library.

Word uses SharePoint Server 2007 to act as the document library and to manage workflows. SharePoint Server 2007 is a set of enterprise-level applications designed to help users manage business content and processes. These applications reside on a server that's available to all of the users in the workflow.

Do it!

C-1: Discussing workflows

Questions and answers

1 What's a workflow?

2 What features of a workflow help to streamline the collaboration process?

3 What application does Microsoft Office Word 2007 use to create workflows?

4 How does creating a workflow differ from creating a document workspace?

Comparing document versions

Explanation

When a reviewer edits a copy of your document, you can compare the edited version side-by-side with the original by using the Compare feature in Word.

To compare two versions of a document:

1. Open the original.
2. Activate the Review tab.
3. Click Compare and select Compare. The Compare Documents dialog box opens.
4. In the Original document list, select the original file.
5. In the Revised document list, select the edited version.
6. Click OK. The document window displays four panes, as shown in Exhibit 3-9.

   - The Reviewing pane includes a list of all changes and who made them.
   - The Compared Document pane displays the original document with highlighted changes accompanied by change bars.
   - The Original Document pane displays your unchanged original.
   - The Revised Document pane displays the edited version of the file, with its changes already implemented.

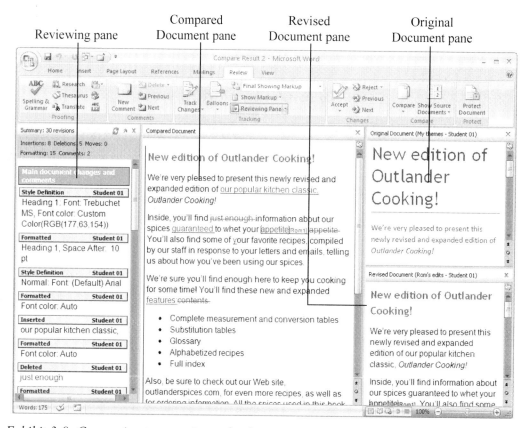

Exhibit 3-9: Comparing two versions of a document

New Word features   **3–19**

Do it!

C-2: Comparing two versions of a document

Here's how	Here's why
1 Start Word	
Open My themes	(From the current unit folder.) You'll compare this document to one that's been reviewed by an Outlander co-worker.
2 Activate the Review tab	
Click **Compare** and select **Compare...**	To display two versions of the document. The Compare Documents dialog box appears.
3 In the Original document list, select **My themes**	Original document My themes La**b**el changes with To specify the active document as the original.
4 Beside the Revised document list, click	(The Browse for Revised button.) The Open dialog box appears.
Navigate to the current unit folder	If necessary.
Select **Rom's edits**	**R**evised document Rom's edits La**b**el changes with Student 01 To specify the revised document. The "Label changes with" box is automatically populated with the user name included in the revised document's file attributes.
Click **Open**	To close the dialog box.
5 Click **More**	Comparison settings ☑ Insertions and deletions ☑ Tables ☑ Mo**v**es ☑ Headers and footers ☑ Comments ☑ Footnotes and en**d**notes ☑ **F**ormatting ☑ Te**x**tboxes ☑ Case changes ☑ Fiel**d**s ☑ White s**p**ace Show changes Show changes at: Show changes in: ○ **C**haracter level ○ Original documen**t** ◉ **W**ord level ○ Revised document ◉ New doc**u**ment To view the comparison options available.
Click **OK**	The document window is divided into four panes, as shown in Exhibit 3-9.

6	In the Tracking group, click the arrow beside Reviewing Pane and verify that Reviewing Pane Vertical is selected	To display the Reviewing Pane on the left side of the screen.
7	In the Compare group, click **Show Source Documents** and verify that Show Both is selected	To show both the original and the revised versions of the document.
8	Observe the pane on the left	The Summary pane lists all changes made to the original document. Each change is headed by a divider that displays the type of change and the name of the reviewer.
9	Observe the pane on the top right	The Original Document pane displays the document in its unchanged state. Scroll bars can be used to view the entire document.
10	Observe the pane on the bottom right	The Revised Document pane displays the document that was edited by the reviewer, in the "after" state—only the changes display.
11	Observe the pane in the center	The Compared Document pane displays both the original content of the document and the changes made by the reviewer—a "before and after" view of the document.
12	Close the Summary pane, the Original Document pane, and the Revised Document pane	(Click the Close box in the title bar of each.) Only the Compare Document pane should be visible.
	In the Changes group, click the arrow beneath Accept	You'll create a new document that incorporates the changes.
	Select **Accept All Changes in Document**	
13	Select Rom's comment	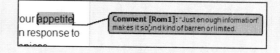
	In the Comments group, click the arrow next to Delete and select **Delete All Comments in Document**	To remove the reviewer's comments.
14	Save the file as **My themes2**	

Static documents

Explanation

You can save a Word file as a *static* document. A static document is one that can't be changed. Saving to a static document format provides two major advantages for sharing the file with others:

- Users who receive a static document don't need to have Word installed to read it. Static documents use viewers that can be downloaded free of charge.
- A static document is a snapshot of the original Word document and can't be altered. The author can be certain that the document content remains unchanged before passing it on.

You can save a file to either of two static document formats:

- XPS—Files saved in Microsoft's XML-based .xps format can be viewed using Internet Explorer. (The XML Paper Specification Essentials Pack must be downloaded and installed.) An XPS file is shown in Exhibit 3-10.
- PDF—Files saved in Adobe's .pdf format can be viewed with the Adobe Acrobat Reader application.

To save a Word file as a static document:

1. Update the document.
2. From the Office Button menu, click the arrow beside Save As.
3. Choose PDF or XPS to open the Publish as PDF or XPS dialog box.
4. Edit the file name, if desired.
5. In the Save as type list, select PDF (*.pdf) or Microsoft XPS (*.xps).
6. Click Publish.

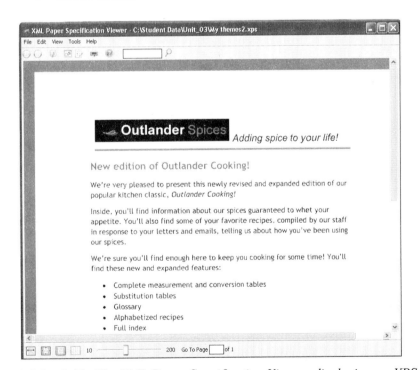

Exhibit 3-10: The XML Paper Specification Viewer, displaying an XPS file

3–22 Office 2007: New Features

Do it!

C-3: Saving a file as a static document

Here's how	Here's why
1 Click the Office Button	To display the menu. You'll save the document in a format that can be viewed but not altered by users.
Display the Save As menu	
Choose **PDF or XPS**	The Save As dialog box opens.
2 In the Save as type box, select **XPS Document**	(If necessary.) The document will be saved in Microsoft's XML Paper Specification format.
Check **Open file after publishing**	If necessary.
3 Click **Publish**	The document is saved in the .xps file format. The XML Paper Specification Viewer opens, and displays the selected file, as shown in Exhibit 3-10.
4 Click anywhere in the document	You can't place the insertion point in the document, nor can you edit any text or objects.
5 Close the XML Viewer	
6 Save and close all open documents	

New Word features   **3–23**

Unit summary: New Word features

Topic A   In this topic, you used **styles** to format text in a document. Then, you created and formatted **charts** and **shapes** in a Word document. Finally, you formatted an entire document using **themes**.

Topic B   In this topic, you inserted **Quick Parts** and **Building Blocks**, and added **custom content** to the Quick Parts gallery and the Building Blocks Organizer.

Topic C   In this topic, you learned how **workflows** can automate the collaboration process for a document developed by a team. Then, you **compared** original and edited versions of a document. Finally, you saved a Word file as a **static** document in either the **XPS** or PDF formats.

Independent practice activity

In this activity you'll apply a Quick Style to a document, format an existing chart, and apply a Theme. Next, you'll save a Building Block as a custom Quick Part and apply it to a document. Finally, you'll save the document in a static format.

1 Open Practice in the current unit folder.

2 Save the document as **My practice**.

3 Format the first line using the **Subtitle** style. (*Hint*: Use the Styles gallery group.)

4 Format the chart to use columns instead of a line. (*Hint*: Click the chart border to select it and use the Change Chart Type button on the Design tab.)

5 Apply the **Metro** theme to the document. (*Hint*: Activate the Page Layout tab and click Themes to display the gallery.)

6 Compare your results to Exhibit 3-11.

7 Update and close the document.

8 Open Closing.

9 Select all of the text in the document.

10 Create a building block from this text. Edit the Name box to read **Closing**, and choose **AutoText** from the Gallery list. Enter **Jake's letter closing** as a description.

11 Close Closing without saving your changes.

12 Open Letter.

13 Insert Jake's letter closing at the end of the document. (*Hint*: Use the Building Blocks Organizer.)

14 Save the document as **My letter**, and close it.

15 Close Word. When prompted, don't save changes to the Building Blocks template.

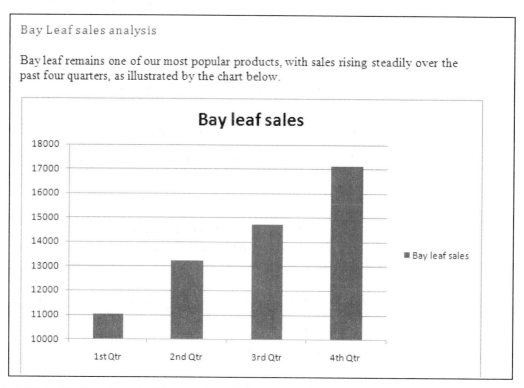

Exhibit 3-11: The chart in My practice after step 5 in the Independent practice activity

Review questions

1 Which of the following can be defined as sets of formatting options that define the appearance of recurring text components?

   A Themes

   B Styles

   C Galleries

   D Toolbars

2 Which of the following statements are true about charts in Word? (Choose all that apply.)

   A You can't edit charts that have been inserted in Word.

   B You must use Excel data to create a chart in Word.

   C Inserted charts are based on Excel worksheets.

   D In the Illustrations group, click Chart to create a chart.

New Word features **3–25**

3 Which of the following are true about themes? (Choose all that apply.)

A Themes provide a way to maintain a consistent look for your documents.

B Themes are available only in Word.

C Themes are sets of colors, fonts, and effects that can be applied to an entire document.

D Themes affect the appearance of tables.

4 The Quick Parts menu used to insert properties and fields in a document. True or false?

5 Building Blocks are a library of reusable components, such as cover pages, headers and footers, page numbers, tables, and other document elements? True or false?

6 What's required before you can use a workflow in Word?

A SharePoint Server 2007

B Exchange Server 2007

C Groove Server 2007

D Forms Server 2007

7 Which feature is used to compare an edited version of a document to the original for the purpose of accepting or rejecting changes?

A Compatibility Checker

B Spelling Checker

C Compare

D Building Blocks Organizer

8 Which static document formats does Word support?

A XPS

B PDF

C TXT

D XML

3–26 Office 2007: New Features

Unit 4
New Excel features

Unit time: 60 minutes

Complete this unit, and you'll know how to:

A Discuss the new worksheet size capabilities.

B Create and format charts, and create reports from existing worksheets.

C Create and format tables, use structured referencing in formulas, name tables, and create functions with the [#ThisRow] function.

D Create and format PivotTables.

E Discuss sharing worksheets by using Excel Services.

4–2 Office 2007: New Features

Topic A: Larger worksheet size

Explanation

You can create much larger worksheets in Excel 2007 than you could in any previous version of Excel.

Worksheet rows and columns

Excel now supports many more rows and columns, as shown in the table that follows.

Version	Columns	Rows	Cells
Excel 2003	256	65,536	16 million
Excel 2007	16,000	1 million	16 billion

The speed with which a computer can recalculate one of the new, massive worksheets might be limited by the machine's RAM, processor speed, or storage space. To help manage the processing load of recalculating a massive worksheet, Excel 2007 has been engineered to take advantage of the processing power in newer dual-processor PCs and multithreading in processor chipsets.

Do it!

A-1: Discussing worksheet size

Questions and answers

1 What was the limitation on worksheet size in Microsoft Office Excel 2003?

2 What's the new worksheet capacity in Microsoft Office Excel 2007?

3 How do these additional cells affect performance?

4 What hardware considerations might limit worksheet capacity?

Topic B: Charts and reports

Explanation

The charting engine has been rewritten for Excel 2007, and new features make it easier to create printed reports directly from worksheet data.

Charts

You can quickly create charts in Excel by using the features of the new user interface. Excel supplies standard chart types, or you can create your own custom chart type.

Excel no longer prompts you to create a chart as either an embedded object or on its own sheet. By default, a chart appears on the current worksheet as a free-floating graphic object that can be dragged and resized, or pasted to another sheet as needed.

To create a chart:

1. Select the data to be charted. Include column or row headings, if desired.
2. Activate the Insert tab.
3. In the Charts group, as shown in Exhibit 4-1, click the type of chart you'd like to create. A gallery of chart styles appears.
4. Select a style from the chart gallery. The chart displays on the worksheet.

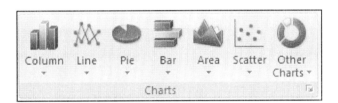

Exhibit 4-1: The Charts group

4-4   Office 2007: New Features

Do it!

B-1:   Creating a chart

Here's how	Here's why
1 Start Microsoft Excel 2007	
2 Open Charts	(From the current unit folder.) This workbook contains some simple data from which you'll create charts.
Save the workbook as **My charts**	In the current unit folder.
3 Select A3:E7	This is the range for which you'll create a chart.
4 Activate the Insert tab	
In the Charts group, click **Column**	To open the gallery of column chart types.
5 Observe the other chart types	Click the Line, Pie, Bar, and Area buttons to see galleries of other available chart types.
Move the pointer over the thumbnails in the galleries	To see the Smart Tooltip that displays for each.
6 Click **Column**	To begin a column chart.
Select **3-D Clustered Column**	 To insert a chart in the worksheet that displays the selected data.

Chart elements

Explanation   Selecting a chart causes three contextual tabs to appear: Design, Layout, and Format. You can use the options on these three tabs to change the appearance of a chart after you've created it.

Galleries of layouts and styles in the tabs make it easy to select from predefined chart designs. Or you can use the individual commands and menus to customize your chart.

Do it!

B-2:   Adding a chart title

Here's how	Here's why
1 Observe the Ribbon	The Ribbon displays the Design, Layout, and Format tabs under Chart Tools.
2 Activate the Layout tab	The Layout tab provides selections for customizing your chart and its elements.

New Excel features **4–5**

3 In the Labels group, click **Chart Title**

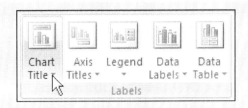

To display the gallery of chart titles.

Select **Above Chart** — To insert a title above the columns in the chart.

4 Select **Chart Title**

The title text is editable.

Edit the text to read **Outlander Spices**

Click anywhere on the chart

To deselect the title.

5 Point to the border around the chart — The pointer changes to a four-sided arrow.

Drag the chart down and to the right — (If necessary.) To move the chart so that you can see the data in A3:E7.

6 Edit B7 to read **500** — To change the value of Julie George's Qtr 1 data.

Observe the chart — Changing the data changed the chart. The column that was the tallest is now the shortest.

Click — (The Undo button is on the Quick Access toolbar.) To return cell B7 to its original value. The chart reflects the change.

7 Update the workbook

Explanation

Formatting a chart

You can use the Format tab to change the way that data is presented in the chart. For example, you can change the default colors used in the chart, add a label to a data series, add titles to the vertical and horizontal axes, or change the scale of the vertical and horizontal axes.

Do it!

B-3: Modifying the chart format

Here's how	Here's why
1 Select the chart	If necessary, to activate the Chart Tools tabs.
Activate the Format tab	You'll format some of the objects on this chart.
2 In the Current Selection group, click the arrow, as indicated	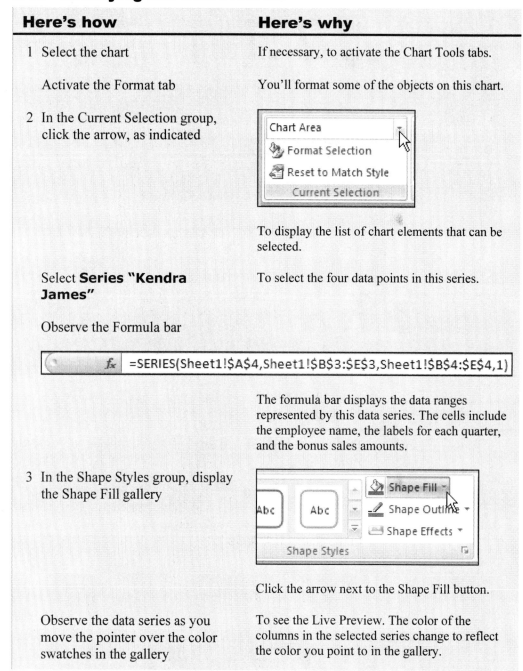
	To display the list of chart elements that can be selected.
Select **Series "Kendra James"**	To select the four data points in this series.
Observe the Formula bar	
=SERIES(Sheet1!$A$4,Sheet1!$B$3:$E$3,Sheet1!$B$4:$E$4,1)	
	The formula bar displays the data ranges represented by this data series. The cells include the employee name, the labels for each quarter, and the bonus sales amounts.
3 In the Shape Styles group, display the Shape Fill gallery	
	Click the arrow next to the Shape Fill button.
Observe the data series as you move the pointer over the color swatches in the gallery	To see the Live Preview. The color of the columns in the selected series change to reflect the color you point to in the gallery.

New Excel features **4–7**

4 Under Theme Colors, select **Orange, Accent 6**	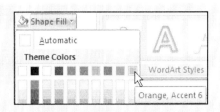
	To give the columns for this data series an orange color.
5 Select **Series "Michael Springer"**	From the Current Selection group.
In the chart, click the column for the Qtr2 data point	To select just that data point in the data series.
Right-click the Qtr2 data point and select **Add Data Label**	
	To display the value of the data point at the top of the column.
6 Activate the Layout tab	You'll label the vertical axis.
In the Labels group, click **Axis Titles**	To display the axis title menu choices.
Choose **Primary Vertical Axis Title, Rotated Title**	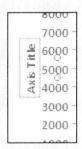
	To insert a rotated title along the vertical axis. The label Axis Title appears.
7 In the chart, click **Axis Title**	To select the editable text.
Edit the text to read **Bonus Sales in Dollars**	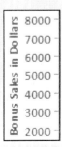

8	In the Axes group, click **Axes**	You'll change the increments for the dollars on the vertical axis.
	Choose **Primary Vertical Axis, More Primary Vertical Axis Options...**	The Format Axis dialog box opens. The Axis Options category settings display by default.
9	Beside Major unit, select **Fixed**	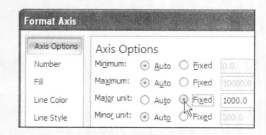
		To change the automatic numbering for the increments.
	Beside Major unit, edit the box to read **2000**	
		To measure the vertical axis in increments of 2000 instead of the default.
	Click **Close**	To close the Format Axis dialog box and apply the change. The vertical axis is selected.
10	Click anywhere on the worksheet	To deselect the chart.
	Observe the chart	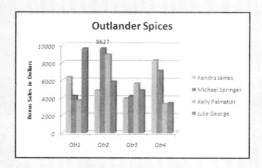
		The spacing of the increments on the vertical axis makes the chart look less cluttered and easier to read.
11	Update and close the workbook	

New Excel features **4–9**

Page Layout view and white space

Explanation   You might need to present worksheet data in printed form. Excel 2007 has made it easy to insert report formatting and page elements.

Page Layout view and Page Break Preview display the current worksheet as it would appear on a printed page. This makes it easy to visualize the printed report, so you can arrange or format data as needed. To switch views, click the desired view button on the right side of the Status bar at the bottom of the window.

White space

While in Page Layout View, you can display white space on the screen to visualize the worksheet as it would appear on a printed page, as shown in Exhibit 4-2.

To display or hide white space and header and footer fields, click the area between the column heading and the first row of the worksheet.

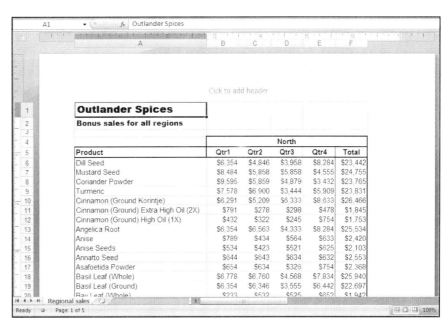

Exhibit 4-2: Page Layout View with white space displayed

Do it!   **B-4: Changing the page layout and adding print titles**

Here's how	Here's why
1 Open Pages	(From the current unit folder.) You'll prepare the worksheet to be printed as a paper report.
Save the file as **My pages**	In the current unit folder.
2 Activate the View tab	
3 In the Workbook Views group, click **Page Layout**	

4	In the Zoom group, click **Zoom**	The Zoom dialog box appears.
	Edit the Custom box to read **65**	
		To reduce the magnification of the worksheet display.
	Click **OK**	To zoom out to 65% magnification.
5	Observe the page layout	The worksheet displays individual pages as they'll appear when printed. You'll correct problems with the layout of the pages.
6	Activate the Page Layout tab	
	In the Page Setup group, click **Print Titles**	The Page Setup dialog box appears. The Sheet tab is activated by default. You'll designate some rows and some columns to appear on every page.
	At the end of the Rows to repeat at top box, click the Collapse button, as indicated	
		The Page Setup - Rows to repeat at top dialog box appears.
	Select rows 1 through 5	
		To enter the rows to print at the top of every page. A dashed line surrounds the selected rows.
7	Observe the Page Setup – Rows to repeat at top box	**Page Setup - Rows to repeat at top:** $1:$5
		Rows 1 through 5 will be repeated at the top of each page.
	Click	(The Expand dialog button is in the Page Setup - Rows to repeat at top dialog box.) To expand the Page Setup dialog box.

8	Select column A as the print title	(Click the Collapse button beside Columns to repeat at left. Then select column A, and click the Expand dialog button to return to the Page Setup dialog box.) To repeat the entire column at the left side of each page.
	Click **OK**	To close the Page Setup dialog box.
9	Observe the pages in the page layout view	The first page displays the column that will repeat and the data columns that will print on that page. The second page (to its right) appears narrower, because it displays only the data columns that will print on that page (F:I). The totals column for the North region spills over onto page two.
10	Select columns B:Z	You'll reduce the width of the columns, so that the data for each region appears on one page.
11	Point to the right edge of column Z, as indicated	
		The pointer changes to a double-sided arrow.
	Drag to the left	To reduce the column size for all the selected columns. As you drag, a Tooltip displays the column width in inches and pixels.
	Set the column width to between **70** and **80** pixels	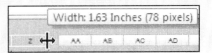
		To make the columns narrow enough so that a region's data appears on a single page but wide enough to display the totals at the bottom of each column.
12	Click the area between the column heading and the first row of the worksheet	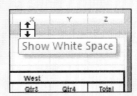
		To display white space. The pages appear as they'll look when printed. Placeholders for headers and footers display on each page.
	Zoom to **100%**	Click the Zoom level on the View tab, or drag the slider on the Status bar to 100%.
13	Press CTRL + HOME	To select A1. Compare your screen to Exhibit 4-2.

Adding headers and footers

Explanation

You can also add page elements, such as print titles, headers, and footers. While in Page Layout View, headers and footers appear as defined boxes on a page. Selecting a header or footer box activates the Header & Footer Tools Design tab. From here, you can insert page number fields, such as current page or total number of pages.

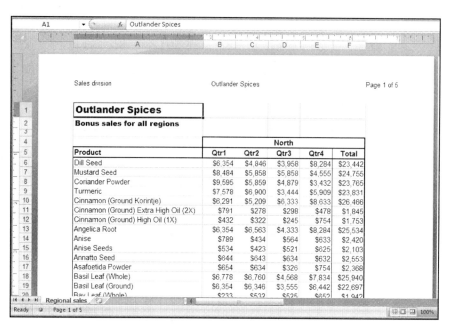

Exhibit 4-3: Page Layout View showing the new headers

Do it!

B-5: Adding a header

Here's how	Here's why
1 Observe the top of any page	A placeholder appears for a header.
Point to **Click to add header**	
Click the center section and enter **Outlander Spices**	The header is divided into left, right, and center sections.
	To add header text that's centered on the page. The Header & Footer Tools Design tab is activated.
2 Press SHIFT + TAB	To move to the left header box.
Enter **Sales division**	
	To add header text that's aligned to the left side of the page.

3 Press `TAB` twice	To move to the right header box. You'll add a header that combines text and predefined elements.
4 Type **Page**	To begin a page numbering element.
Press `SPACEBAR`	To place a space between the word and the element that will follow it.
On the Design tab, in the Header & Footer Elements group, click **Page Number**	

To insert an element that prints the current page number.

5 Press `SPACEBAR`	
Type **of**	
Press `SPACEBAR`	
In the Header & Footer elements group, click **Number of Pages**	

Page &[Page] of &[Pages]

To insert an element that prints the total number of pages in the workbook.

6 Select A1	To deselect the header and move to the first page of the worksheet.
Observe the header	The right-side element reads "Page 1 of 5" instead of the header code. Compare your screen to the one shown in Exhibit 4-3.
7 From the Office Button menu, choose **Print**, **Print Preview**	To display the worksheet in Print Preview mode.
8 Zoom in on the header	Point to the header and click.
Zoom out of the page	Click anywhere on the page.
Scroll through the pages	To see that each region fits on a single page.
Click **Close Print Preview**	To return to the worksheet.
9 On the View tab, click **Normal**	To switch from Page Layout View to Normal view. The page divisions, headers, and other layout items no longer appear.
Update and close the worksheet	

4–14 Office 2007: New Features

Topic C: Table options

Explanation

When you define a range as a table, Excel formats it and automatically enables filtering. It also changes the way you add to a table and the way formulas reference its cells.

Creating tables

You can convert a range of data to a table in three ways. With a cell within the data selected:

- On the Home tab, in the Styles group, select a table style from the Format as Table gallery.
- On the Insert tab, in the Tables group, click Table.
- Press Ctrl+T.

Formatting tables

When you create a table, the Table Tools appear, and the Design tab is automatically activated. You can format the table by choosing options on this tab.

Options in the Table Style Options group can format rows and columns:

- The Header Row and Totals Row options determine whether Excel formats the top and bottom row and affect how Excel references columns in formulas (as named ranges or as individual cells).
- The First Column and Last Column options determine whether Excel formats the leftmost and rightmost columns differently from the interior ones. Not all table styles apply first and last column formatting, so it might not make a difference whether this option is checked or not.
- The Banded Rows or Banded columns options apply fill colors to alternating rows or columns, which can make them easier to differentiate.

Choosing a table style from the Table Styles group changes the color scheme and borders. If you've already formatted the header and/or left column prior to creating the table, your original formatting remains, so only the body of the table receives new formatting. If you want to return to the formatting you applied prior to creating the table, select the first table style, None. This table style doesn't appear in the Format as Table gallery. You can apply it only after the table has been created.

Do it!

C-1: Creating and formatting a table

Here's how	Here's why
1 Open Product	(From the current unit folder.) This workbook contains sheets with inventory and sales information.
Save the workbook as **My product**	
2 Select any cell in the range A6:C19	You don't need to select the entire table's range; Excel will attempt to determine it automatically.
3 Activate the Insert tab	

New Excel features   **4–15**

4 In the Tables group, click **Table**

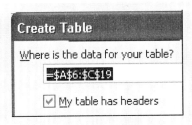

To open the Create Table dialog box. The selected range is correct, and the table has headers, so you can accept the defaults.

Click **OK**

To close the dialog box and create the table. Next, you'll modify the default formatting of the table.

5 Select a single cell within the table

To deselect the table, so you can view its formatting without highlighted cells.

6 Verify that the Table Tools Design tab is activated

Excel automatically activates this tab when you select a cell within a newly created table.

In the Table Style Options group, check **First Column**

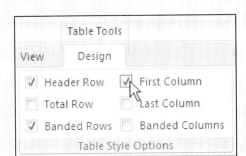

To format the first column per the table style. Observe that in addition to the color formatting, the text becomes bold.

Clear **Banded Rows**

To turn off the alternating row fill colors. You decide you'd prefer the table formatted just as it was prior to defining the range as a table.

7 In the Table Styles group, scroll to the top of the gallery and select **None**

To remove the table formatting. The bold first column formatting disappears, because the None table style overrides the Table Style Options tab formatting.

To the table, apply **Table Style Medium 4**

In the Medium section of the Table Styles group.

8 Update the workbook

4–16 Office 2007: New Features

Table AutoExpansion

Explanation

When you type in a cell adjacent to a table, Excel automatically adds it to the table and formats the top row or left column cell to match. This AutoCorrect option is called *Table AutoExpansion*, which you can change, if desired, by clicking the AutoCorrect Options button that appears.

If you want to add or delete several rows and columns at once, you can click Resize Table in the Properties group on the Table Tools Design tab, then specify a new range for the table.

Do it!

C-2:   Working with Table AutoExpansion

Here's how	Here's why
1 In D6, enter **Total value**	
	When you press Enter, Excel automatically formats the column to match the table style. In this case, the existing table cells had borders applied before you created the table, and this is not copied to the new column. An AutoCorrect Options button appears.
Click the AutoCorrect Options button as shown	
	To display options for the automatic action just taken.
Observe the options in the list	You can undo the automatic expansion of the table, stop automatically expanding tables, or control all AutoCorrect options.
Press (ESC)	To close the list.
2 In A20, type **Cinnamon** and press (TAB)	To create a new row. Excel automatically expands the table.
In B20, type **10** and press (TAB)	The value is given the formatting used by the rest of the column.
In C20, enter **400**	
3 Update the workbook	

Structured referencing

Explanation

Excel applies *structured referencing* within formulas when you create a table. Structured referencing automatically names table columns based on their headings (the values in the top row), then uses those names in formulas whenever possible.

For example, if you begin creating a formula within a table, and click another table cell within the same row to reference it, Excel inserts that cell's column name instead of the A1-style reference, as it would normally use, as shown in Exhibit 4-4.

Exhibit 4-4: Formula contains table column reference

To use structured referencing when typing formulas, type [to begin a column reference. You can also type a formula with an A1-style cell reference, and Excel won't replace it with a column name, so you can still create traditional formulas, if desired.

When you press Enter, the AutoCorrect function fills the formula to all other cells in the column. If the formula references a column name, it appears the same in each cell. Formulas with structured referencing are easier to read and less prone to errors—because each cell can contain the exact same formula, it would be more difficult to change one accidentally.

The Total row

A table can include a Total row at the bottom. Each of its cells can hold a function to summarize the data in the column above. By default, cells in the Total row use the SUBTOTAL function, which, depending on its arguments, can act like SUM, AVERAGE, or others.

The SUBTOTAL function always displays the correct value, if you apply a filter to one or more columns. For example, if you apply a filter that hides all but two rows, as shown in Exhibit 4-5, the SUBTOTAL function in the Total row sums just those values and doesn't include the hidden ones.

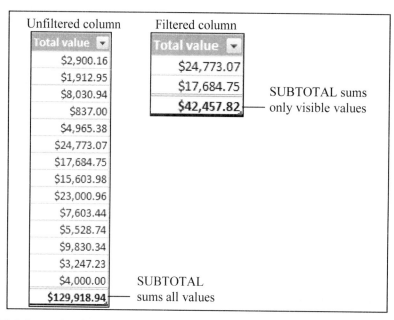

Exhibit 4-5: The SUBTOTAL function in the Totals row operates only on visible cells

Excel creates a Total row automatically, if you select a cell directly below the table and create a formula using the AutoSum button, or if you check Total Row in the Quick Style Options group on the Table Tools Design tab.

Do it!

C-3: Applying structured referencing

Here's how	Here's why
1 In D7, type =	To begin creating a formula. Don't press Enter.
Click B7	To add a reference to the formula. Unlike standard ranges, which place A1-style cell references, Excel places a reference to the cell's column [Unit price], when you add it by clicking a cell within a table.
Type *	To enter the multiplication operator.
Click C7	
=Table1[[#This Row],[Unit price]]*Table1[[#This Row],[Qty in stock]]	
	To add [#ThisRow],[Qty in stock] to the formula.

2	Press ⏎ ENTER	To complete the formula. AutoCorrect automatically fills the formula to create a Calculated Column.
	Observe the formula in D8	The formula in this cell, and in each one in the column, is the same as the one you entered. All refer to the column name, not to individual cells within.
3	Activate the Table Tools Design tab	If necessary.
	In the Table Style Options group, check **Total Row**	To add a Total row at the bottom of the table.
	Select D21 and observe the formula within	The formula =SUBTOTAL(109,[Total value]) calculates the sum of the visible cells in the column.
4	From the menu for D21, choose **Average**, and observe the formula	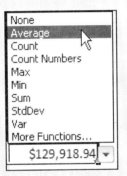 The cell displays the average value. The first argument of the function changes from 109 (which represented Sum) to 101 (which represents Average).
	From the menu for D21, choose **Sum**	To reset the formula to calculate the sum.
5	Select C21	
	Activate the Formulas tab	
	Click **AutoSum**	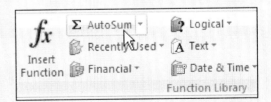 (Click the button, not the menu.) Excel creates a SUBTOTAL function to sum the column.
6	In A6, click the AutoFilter arrow next to Product	To display the sort and list criteria. You'll display only spices with names beginning with the letter B.

7 Choose **Text Filters, Begins With...**	To open the Custom AutoFilter dialog box. In the upper-left list, the first comparison operator, "begins with," is selected.
In the upper-right box, enter **B**	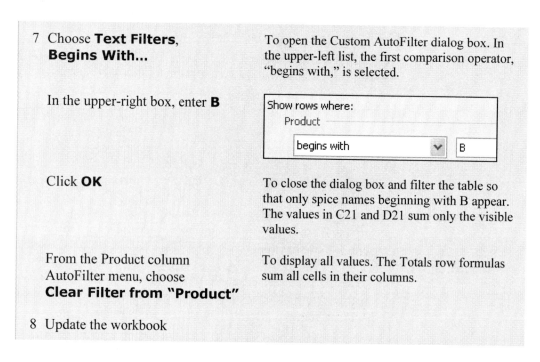
Click **OK**	To close the dialog box and filter the table so that only spice names beginning with B appear. The values in C21 and D21 sum only the visible values.
From the Product column AutoFilter menu, choose **Clear Filter from "Product"**	To display all values. The Totals row formulas sum all cells in their columns.
8 Update the workbook	

Table names

Explanation

When you create a table, Excel automatically assigns it a name (Table1 for the first table in the workbook, Table2 for the second, etc.) If you create a formula in a cell outside the table that references columns within the table, Excel uses structured referencing to insert the table name and column name in the formula, as shown in Exhibit 4-6. Formulas within the table don't use the name by default, just as most formulas don't include the worksheet name unless it's necessary.

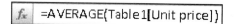

Exhibit 4-6: A formula that refers to the Unit Price column in the Table1 table

You can edit the table's name in the Properties group on the Table Tools Design tab. Formulas that refer to the table update automatically when you change the table name.

Do it!

C-4: Creating and using table names

Here's how	Here's why
1 In B4, type **=AVERAGE(**	(Don't press Enter.) Excel anticipates the formula that you might want.
2 Select B7:B20	To select the Unit price column. The formula appears as shown in Exhibit 4-6.
Press ⏎ ENTER	To enter the formula. If you Auto Fill the cell to the right, the next cell's formula will contain the adjacent table column's name.
3 Auto Fill B4 to the right	To copy the formula to C4.
From the Auto Fill Options menu, choose **Fill Without Formatting**	Averages: $25.89 362
	To remove the currency formatting from C4.
Select C4 and observe the formula	*fx* =AVERAGE(Table1[Qty in stock])
	The formula references Table1[Qty in stock].
4 Select any cell within the table	To display the Table Tools Design tab.
Activate the Design tab	
5 In the Properties group, edit the Table Name box to read **InventoryTable**	Table Name: InventoryTable Resize Table Properties
	Don't enter a space between words.
Select B4	*fx* =AVERAGE(InventoryTable[Unit price])
	The formula now references InventoryTable instead of Table1.
6 Update the workbook	

Functions tabulating row values

Explanation

Some Excel functions expect the arguments to be a range of cells. For example, the SUM function acts upon a range of values, not just one. Therefore, an argument, such as a table column name, is valid for the SUM function, then =SUM([January] is the equivalent of =SUM(C5:C14).

At times, however, you might want to use a table column name within a function but reference only a single row. For example, if you want to sum the values across a table row, you don't want to sum all the values for all of the rows.

To address this issue, you can insert a special [#This Row] argument within formulas. Exhibit 4-7 shows this argument within a cell that sums the values within one row of the January through April columns of a table. While you can type this argument, the easiest way to insert it is to use the AutoSum button to create the formula. Excel inserts it automatically.

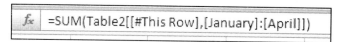

Exhibit 4-7: A function to sum a single row should include [#This Row]

	A	B	C	D	E	F	G
1	Outlander Spices						
2	Bonus sales report						
3							
4	Product	Region	January	February	March	April	Total
5	Cinnamon	East	$20,345	$29,196	$17,990	$18,158	$85,689
6	Cinnamon (Ground)	East	$26,400	$34,879	$15,541	$22,731	$99,551
7	Anise Seeds	East	$2,253	$2,139	$11,312	$20,218	$35,923
8	Annatto Seed	East	$2,146	$1,871	$11,771	$24,181	$39,969
9	Cassia	East	$18,772	$18,780	$19,426	$23,273	$80,251
10	Cinnamon	North	$2,511	$2,158	$17,611	$25,166	$47,446
11	Cinnamon (Ground)	North	$3,829	$1,753	$17,314	$17,924	$40,820
12	Anise Seeds	North	$3,190	$2,471	$17,975	$25,573	$49,209
13	Annatto Seed	North	$3,248	$3,253	$13,839	$18,336	$38,676
14	Cassia	North	$2,301	$2,468	$17,648	$23,818	$46,235

G5: =SUM(Table2[[#This Row],[January]:[April]])

Exhibit 4-8: Filling the formula containing the [#This Row] argument

New Excel features   **4–23**

Do it!   ## C-5:   Creating functions with [#This Row]

Here's how	Here's why
1 Activate the Sales sheet	You'll convert this sheet's data to a table, then add a formula in a new column.
Select a cell within A4:F14 and define the range as a table	Activate the Insert tab, then click Table in the Tables group. Click OK to accept the defaults.
2 In G4, enter **Total**	Excel adds this column to the table automatically.
3 Activate the Home tab	If necessary.
With G5 selected, click **AutoSum** in the Editing group	
	To add a formula that sums the values from the January through April columns for row 5. The formula appears as the one shown in Exhibit 4-7.
Press ⏎ ENTER	To create the formula and automatically fill it to the remaining rows in the column. Compare your screen to the one shown in Exhibit 4-8.
4 Select G5	If necessary.
Edit the formula to read =SUM(Table2[[January]:[April]])	(Delete the text [#This Row], from the formula.) When you press Enter, all cells in the column display the result $563,768, because all are summing all of the values in the columns, not just the values to the cell's left.
In the Quick Access toolbar, click **Undo Fill**	To return to the original formula in the filled cells.
Click **Undo Typing**	To return all cells to the intended formula.
5 Update and close the workbook	

Topic D: PivotTables

Explanation

Creating and working with PivotTables is easier in Excel 2007 than in previous versions.

Creating a PivotTable

To create a PivotTable:

1. Select any cell in a data range that includes a heading for each column in the top row.
2. Activate the Insert tab.
3. In the Tables group, click the PivotTable button, or click the PivotTable list and select PivotTable to open the Create PivotTable dialog box.
4. In the Table/Range box, select the range that contains the data to be used in the PivotTable.
5. Select the location for the PivotTable. You can place the PivotTable in a new or existing worksheet. Click OK to create the PivotTable. Your screen resembles the one shown in Exhibit 4-9.

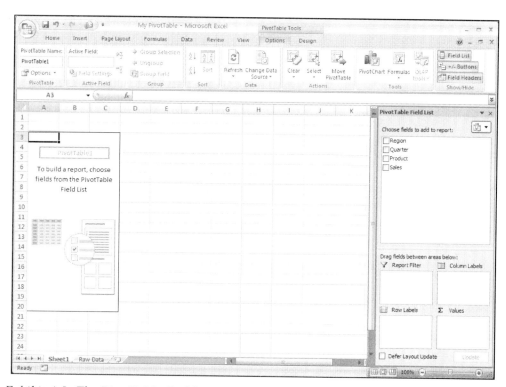

Exhibit 4-9: The PivotTable Field List pane

The PivotTable Field List

When you create a PivotTable, the PivotTable Field List displays as a pane in the right side of the Excel window, as shown in Exhibit 4-9. You can drag fields within the PivotTable Field list to assign them to parts of the PivotTable and specify how your data is arranged. You can change the data view by dragging fields to other areas in the PivotTable Field List.

The PivotTable Tools tabs

When a PivotTable is selected, contextual tabs display, as shown in Exhibit 4-10. You can use the PivotTable Tools Options and Design tabs to modify the content and format of the PivotTable.

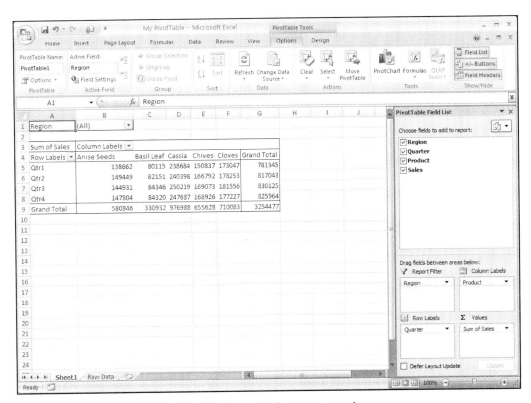

Exhibit 4-10: The PivotTable after fields have been assigned

4–26   Office 2007: New Features

Do it!

D-1: Creating and formatting PivotTables

Here's how	Here's why
1 Open PivotTable	(From the current unit folder.) The PivotTable file contains the sales details for several products. You'll use the data in this worksheet to create a PivotTable.
Save the workbook as **My PivotTable**	In the current unit folder.
2 Select any cell in the range A5:D105	You'll create a PivotTable based on this range. If you select a cell within the range of the source data, you won't have to specify the range later.
3 Activate the Insert tab	
4 In the Tables group, click the PivotTable button	
	The Create PivotTable dialog box appears. It prompts you to select the location of the data you want to analyze. You can use an external data source or an Excel worksheet.
Observe the default range	The default is the range it determines automatically from the selected cell.
Observe the default location	You can create the PivotTable in a new worksheet (default) or in an existing worksheet.
Click **OK**	Sheet1 is added as a new worksheet. It displays the layout of the PivotTable, PivotTable Tools Options and Design tabs, and the PivotTable Field List pane, as shown in Exhibit 4-9.
5 From the PivotTable Field List pane, drag **Region** to the Report Filter box, as shown	
	Region appears in cell A1 in the spreadsheet with a dropdown arrow.
Drag **Quarter** to Row Labels	To add Quarter as a row field in the PivotTable.
Drag **Product** to Column Labels	To add Product as a column field.
Drag **Sales** to Σ Values	To add Sales as the values item. The PivotTable shows the sum of the quarterly sales for several products. Compare your screen to the one shown in Exhibit 4-10.
6 Activate the Design tab	You'll change the PivotTable's format.

7	Display the PivotTable Styles gallery	Click the More button on the right side of the gallery.
	Point to a few styles	Live Preview shows you a preview of how the styles will look.
8	Select **Pivot Style Medium 2**	
		Row and column headings are shaded, and the Grand Total row is boldfaced.
	Click anywhere outside the PivotTable	To deselect it. The contextual tabs and the PivotTable Field List pane disappear. You can display them again at any time by clicking within the PivotTable to activate it.
9	Update and close the workbook	

4–28 Office 2007: New Features

Topic E: Excel Services

Explanation

In a team environment, it's often necessary to display the data in an Excel worksheet for a group of users. Excel Services makes it easy to share Excel worksheets. *Excel Services* is an application included in Office SharePoint Server 2007, a set of server-based applications designed for the enterprise environment.

Sharing workbooks

To share a worksheet, you store the original worksheet on SharePoint Server 2007. Excel Services generates an HTML version of the worksheet. Users who have permission rights to the worksheet can then view it in a browser. As with an ordinary Web page, the capabilities of the server are the only limit on the number of users who can view the worksheet.

The browser-based version of the worksheet is intended for display purposes and doesn't support most Excel functions. However, a user can sort and filter data, and change PivotTable views. All of these changes occur in the user's browser-based version of the worksheet. The original Excel worksheet on the server remains unchanged.

Do it!

E-1: Discussing Excel Services for online sharing

Questions and answers

1 What type of application is Excel Services?

2 What's Office SharePoint Server 2007?

3 What does Excel Services do?

4 What functions can users perform on a worksheet opened in Excel Services?

5 Can users make changes to the worksheet?

6 How many users can view the worksheet?

7 Can anyone view worksheets stored on the server?

New Excel features **4–29**

Unit summary: New Excel features

Topic A   In this topic, you learned about the new **worksheet size** capabilities.

Topic B   In this topic, you learned how to create and format **charts**. Then, you learned how to create and format **reports** from existing worksheet data.

Topic C   In this topic, you learned how to create and format **tables**, and to add rows and columns. Then, you learned how to apply **structured referencing** to Excel formulas. Next, you learned how to **name tables**. Finally, you learned how to use the **[#ThisRow]** argument in formulas to reference only a single row in a structured reference.

Topic D   In this topic, you learned how to create **PivotTables** by using the PivotTable Field List task pane. Then, you formatted the PivotTable using the contextual **Options and Design tabs**.

Topic E   In this topic, you learned about the features of **Excel Services** that can be applied to **sharing** HTML versions of worksheets online.

Independent practice activity

In this activity, you'll configure a worksheet to be used as a printed report, then create and format a chart.

1   Open Report and save it as **My report**.

2   Configure the data to print on paper in landscape format. (*Hint*: Use the Page Layout tabs.)

3   Make columns A:B appear on every page. (*Hint*: Zoom out to see more of the data. Then click Print Titles, and select A:B as the columns to repeat at left.)

4   Add a centered header to each page that displays **Outlander Spices** and **Bonus Sales by Region**. (*Hint*: Click the Header section on any page and type the text.)

5   Add a centered footer that displays the current date on each page.

6   Compare your results to the worksheet shown in Exhibit 4-11.

7   Update and close the workbook.

8   Open Data and save the file as **My data**.

9   On the Chart sheet, select only the names and totals. (*Hint*: Use the Ctrl key to select the non-contiguous ranges A3:A7 and F3:F7.)

10   Create a 3-D pie chart for the selected data. Compare your screen to the one shown in Exhibit 4-12.

11   Update and close the workbook.

12   Close Excel 2007.

Outlander Spices
Bonus Sales by Region

Region	Qtr	Dill	Mustard	Coriander	Turmeric	Cinnamon (Korintje)	Cinnamon Oil (2X)	Cinnamon Oil (1X)	Angelica Root	Anise
North	Q1	$6,354	$8,484	$9,595	$7,578	$6,291	$791	$432	$6,354	$789
	Q2	$4,846	$5,858	$5,859	$6,900	$5,209	$278	$322	$6,563	$434
	Q3	$3,958	$5,858	$4,879	$3,444	$6,333	$298	$245	$4,333	$564
	Q4	$8,284	$4,555	$3,432	$5,909	$8,633	$478	$754	$8,284	$633
	Total	$23,442	$24,755	$23,765	$23,831	$26,466	$1,845	$1,753	$25,534	$2,420
South	Q1	$5,235	$9,041	$10,243	$8,457	$9,457	$734	$436	$3,466	$422
	Q2	$6,333	$8,364	$8,925	$2,466	$7,457	$642	$733	$2,662	$624
	Q3	$2,535	$6,349	$5,254	$7,466	$7,545	$345	$634	$6,422	$733
	Q4	$6,242	$2,646	$5,266	$4,666	$8,945	$532	$343	$6,222	$732
	Total	$20,345	$26,400	$29,688	$23,055	$33,404	$2,253	$2,146	$18,772	$2,511
Central	Q1	$8,990	$8,926	$9,827	$8,922	$2,266	$654	$345	$4,632	$574
	Q2	$9,452	$8,922	$6,782	$9,892	$7,225	$643	$633	$7,222	$553
	Q3	$7,222	$9,208	$6,282	$8,902	$3,636	$431	$463	$3,464	$754
	Q4	$3,532	$7,823	$5,798	$9,829	$6,634	$431	$432	$3,462	$277
	Total	$29,196	$34,879	$28,689	$37,545	$19,761	$2,139	$1,871	$18,780	$2,158
East	Q1	$9,012	$11,890	$12,323	$10,234	$9,860	$791	$346	$8,967	$585
	Q2	$6,778	$9,876	$8,932	$9,845	$9,856	$744	$864	$9,677	$898
	Q3	$9,878	$10,244	$6,784	$6,538	$11,333	$644	$754	$4,747	$1,074
	Q4	$10,234	$9,876	$8,446	$9,844	$10,944	$465	$855	$7,474	$636
	Total	$35,902	$41,886	$36,485	$36,461	$41,993	$2,644	$2,819	$30,865	$3,193
West	Q1	$6,354	$8,484	$9,595	$7,578	$6,291	$791	$432	$6,354	$789
	Q2	$4,846	$5,858	$5,859	$6,900	$5,209	$278	$322	$6,563	$434
	Q3	$3,958	$5,858	$4,879	$3,444	$6,333	$298	$245	$4,333	$564
	Q4	$8,284	$4,555	$3,432	$5,909	$8,633	$478	$754	$8,284	$633
	Total	$23,442	$24,755	$23,765	$23,831	$26,466	$1,845	$1,753	$25,534	$2,420
Spice totals		$132,327	$152,675	$142,392	$144,723	$148,090	$10,726	$10,342	$119,485	$12,702

7/7/2006

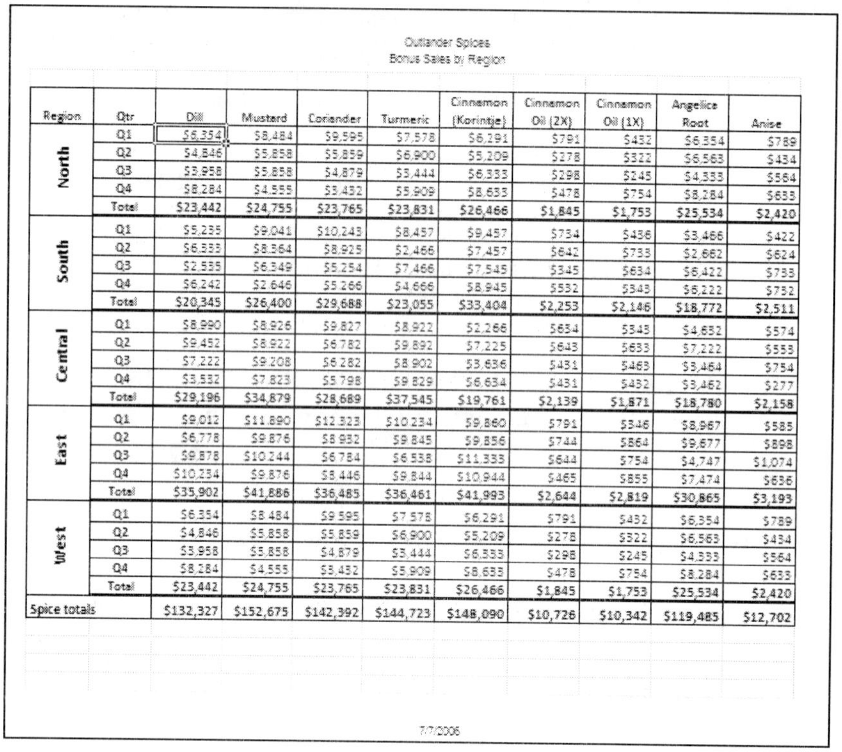

Exhibit 4-11: The worksheet with a header and footer

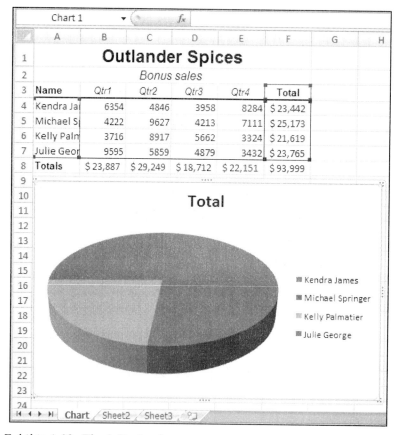

Exhibit 4-12: The 3-D pie chart

Review questions

1 How many cells are supported by Excel 2007?

   A Up to 16 million

   B Less than 16 million

   C Up to 16 billion

   D Over 16 billion

2 What's the first step in creating a chart in Excel 2007?

   A Choose the chart type on the Ribbon.

   B Select the data to be charted.

   C Choose destination cell for the chart.

   D Display the Chart Tools contextual tabs.

3 What Ribbon tabs appear specifically to modify a chart after it's been created? (Choose all that apply.)

   A Design tab

   B Layout tab

   C Format tab

   D Home tab

4 Which of the following displays a worksheet as it would appear on a printed page? (Choose all that apply.)

   A Reading Layout view

   B Normal view

   C Page Layout view

   D Page Break Preview

5 Which of the following is true of a range that has been defined as a table? (Choose all that apply.)

   A Tables are more difficult to format.

   B Filtering of table columns is enabled automatically.

   C Data added to adjacent cells are added to the table automatically.

   D Table names and column names change the way that cells are referenced in formulas.

4–32   Office 2007: New Features

6 The PivotTable Field List is used to assign fields to parts of the PivotTable. True or false?

7 To use Excel Services for sharing worksheets, you must have a _____ Server 2007.

5–1

Unit 5

New PowerPoint features

Unit time: 45 minutes

Complete this unit, and you'll know how to:

A Convert a bulleted list to a diagram, and format the diagram.

B Discuss sharing content with a slide library.

C Create static documents, discuss a team review process, and discuss digital signatures.

D Create custom slide layouts and apply themes.

5–2 Office 2007: New Features

Topic A: Dynamic SmartArt graphics

Explanation

PowerPoint 2007 includes a gallery of *SmartArt* diagrams and graphics that can be used in presentations.

Convert to SmartArt

You can convert a bulleted list of items to a diagram to create a more visual, less text-based slide. Here's how:

1 Click anywhere in the list to select it.
2 Activate the Home tab.
3 In the Paragraph group, click Convert to SmartArt Graphic.
4 Click More SmartArt Graphics. The Choose a SmartArt Graphic dialog box appears, as shown in Exhibit 5-1.
5 In the pane on the left, choose a diagram category.
6 In the center pane, choose a diagram from the gallery. The right pane displays a close-up of the chosen diagram and a brief description.
7 Click OK.

SmartArt graphic categories include those listed in the table that follows.

Category	Description
List	A group of items that doesn't necessarily imply movement or progress.
Process	A linear progression of steps with a beginning and, sometimes, an end.
Cycle	A continuing sequence that doesn't necessarily have a beginning or end.
Hierarchy	A ranking of items in which some are subordinate to others.
Relationship	How individual items relate to each other or to the group.
Matrix	The relationship of parts to the whole.
Pyramid	Hierarchical or foundation-based relationships.

New PowerPoint features 5-3

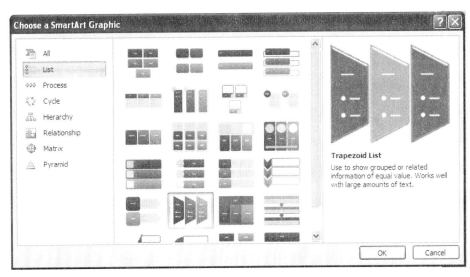

Exhibit 5-1: The Choose a SmartArt Graphic dialog box

5–4 Office 2007: New Features

Do it! **A-1: Converting a bulleted list to SmartArt**

Here's how	Here's why
1 Start Microsoft PowerPoint 2007	
2 Open Project	(From the current unit folder.) This presentation contains a bulleted list that you'll convert to a graphic.
Save the presentation as **My project**	In the current unit folder.
3 Select the fourth slide	The Progress-to-date slide shows a list of accomplishments.
Click anywhere in the list	To select the placeholder.
4 Verify that the Home tab is activated	If necessary.
In the Paragraph group, click [icon]	(The Convert to SmartArt Graphic button.) The Conversion gallery displays.
Choose **More SmartArt Graphics...**	To open the Choose a SmartArt Graphic dialog box.
5 In the left pane, click **List**	To limit the diagrams to those that show item lists.
6 In the center pane, click **Picture Accent List**	
Observe the right pane	The right pane shows a full-color image of the diagram. The text describes the best use of this diagram, as well as the text levels that it's appropriate for.
7 Click **Trapezoid List**	As shown in Exhibit 5-1, this diagram style accommodates large amounts of text.
Click **OK**	To close the dialog box. The bullet list converts to a diagram. A text-entry dialog box appears to the left of the diagram.
8 Click anywhere on the slide	To deselect the diagram and close the text entry box.
9 Update the presentation	

New PowerPoint features   **5–5**

Changing the appearance of a diagram

Explanation   You can manipulate the SmartArt graphics used in diagrams by editing the text in the diagram or by changing the appearance, such as colors and patterns. To do so, click to select the diagram. When you select a diagram, contextual tabs for SmartArt Tools appear. The Design tab includes controls for changing the style and layout of the diagram as a whole. The Format tab can change individual elements within a diagram.

Do it!   ## A-2:   Formatting diagrams

Here's how	Here's why
1 Click the diagram	(If necessary.) To select it. The Text box displays beside it.
In the Text box, click the Close box	
	To close the Text box, while the diagram remains selected.
2 Observe the Ribbon	The SmartArt Tools Design and Format tabs display.
Activate the Design tab	Under SmartArt Tools.
3 In the Layouts group, click the More button, as indicated	
	To display the Layouts gallery.
Move the pointer over the layouts in the gallery	Live preview displays the results on the presentation.
Press ESC	To close the gallery.
4 Display the SmartArt Styles gallery	In the SmartArt Styles group, click the More button at the bottom-right of the list.
Move the pointer over the styles in the gallery	To see the results in Live Preview.
Under 3-D, click **Powder**	To apply this style to the diagram.
5 Update the presentation	

5–6 Office 2007: New Features

Topic B: Slide libraries

Explanation

Office SharePoint Server 2007 is a set of server-based applications designed for the enterprise environment. For PowerPoint, SharePoint makes it possible to create a *slide library* for sharing slides with team members.

Slide libraries and SharePoint Server 2007

The system administrator who manages SharePoint server creates a Web site on the server to act as the slide library and gives read and write permission to you and your team members. When you save a completed presentation to the slide library, SharePoint saves the presentation as individual slides. Any slide can then be reused by other members of your team, when they're preparing their own presentations. When reusing a slide from a library, you can link your copy of the slide to the one in the slide library. If the original author changes the slide, PowerPoint prompts you to update your copy.

Do it!

B-1: Discussing SharePoint Server 2007

Questions and answers
1 What's Office SharePoint Server 2007?
2 How does Office SharePoint Server 2007 interact with PowerPoint 2007?
3 How can Office SharePoint 2007 be used to share presentation content?
4 What if a slide stored in the library changes after you include it in your presentation?

New PowerPoint features **5-7**

Topic C: **Sharing presentations**

Explanation

You can share a presentation by saving it as a static document or by using server technologies to collaborate on it. When you send a presentation, you can attach a digital signature to it.

Static documents

You can save a PowerPoint presentation as a static document. In a static document, each PowerPoint slide is saved as a separate page. Advantages of static documents include:

- Users don't need PowerPoint to read them. Static documents use free viewers.
- A static document can't be altered by those who pass it on.

You can save a file to either of two static document formats:

- XPS—Files saved in Microsoft's XML-based .xps format can be viewed using Internet Explorer. (The XML Paper Specification Essentials Pack must be downloaded and installed.)
- PDF—Files saved in Adobe's .pdf format can be viewed with the Adobe Acrobat Reader.

To save a PowerPoint presentation as a static document:

1 Update the document.
2 Click the Microsoft Office Button and click the arrow beside Save As.
3 Choose PDF or XPS. The Publish as PDF or XPS dialog box appears.
4 Edit the file name, if necessary.
5 In the Save as type list, select PDF (*.pdf) or Microsoft XPS (*.xps).
6 Click Publish.

5–8 Office 2007: New Features

Do it!

C-1: Saving as a static document

Here's how	Here's why
1 From the Microsoft Office Button menu, click the arrow next to **Save As**	To display the Save As choices. You'll save the presentation in a format that can be viewed but not altered by users.
Choose **PDF or XPS**	To open the Publish as PDF or XPS dialog box.
2 In the Save as type list, select **XPS Document**	Save as type: PDF / PDF / XPS Document / Optimize for:
	(If necessary.) The document will be saved in Microsoft's XML Paper Specification format.
Check **Open file after publishing**	(At the bottom of the dialog box.) To specify that the file will open automatically when it's generated. You can open the file at any time by using Internet Explorer.
Click **Publish**	To save the document in the .xps file format. The XML Paper Specification Viewer opens, displaying the file.
3 Click anywhere in the document	You can't place the insertion point in the document, nor can you edit objects.
Page through the document	Each slide is saved to a page.
4 Close the XML Viewer	
5 Close the presentation	

New PowerPoint features **5–9**

Presentation reviews

Explanation

Teams can use PowerPoint and Office server applications to work together to review or collaborate on presentations.

SharePoint Server 2007

An author can use SharePoint 2007 to create a workflow to automate the team review process. A workflow is the review path that a presentation follows before being finalized.

A user selects a predefined workflow from within PowerPoint 2007. Team members automatically receive an e-mail informing them that the presentation is ready for review. When they've finished, they send the original author an e-mail that includes a workflow completion form describing the presentation's status.

Office Groove 2007

Sometimes a linear review process isn't the best way to produce a presentation. Office Groove 2007 is a server application that allows team members to work together on a single copy of a presentation in real-time.

Do it!

C-2: Discussing presentation review processes

Questions and answers

1 What are two methods that a team can use to review a PowerPoint 2007 presentation?

2 What's Office Groove 2007?

3 What's an Office SharePoint Server 2007 workflow?

4 How would an author use an Office SharePoint Server 2007 workflow to initiate the approvals process?

Digital certificates and digital signatures

Explanation

A *digital signature* is an electronic security stamp that's used to authenticate a presentation or another Office document. This helps confirm that the file originated from the person who signed it and that no one has altered it. Digital signatures in PowerPoint 2007 use Microsoft Authenticode technology. To use a digital signature, you need to obtain and install a digital certificate. A *digital certificate* is an attachment that guarantees security for a document.

There are two types of digital certificates: Class 2 and Class 3. A *Class 2* digital certificate is for people who publish software individually. This certificate guarantees the identity of the individual publisher. A *Class 3* digital certificate is for companies that publish software, and it guarantees the identity of the publishing company. In addition, the Class 3 digital certificate guarantees that the company satisfies the minimum financial stability level as stipulated by Dun & Bradstreet Financial Services.

To obtain a digital certificate, you or your organization should submit an application to a commercial certification authority, such as VeriSign Inc. The application can also be submitted to your internal security administrator or an Information Technology professional. You can also create your own digital certificates, called *self-signed projects*, by using the Selfcert.exe tool. However, self-signed projects might be considered unauthenticated and might generate a warning, because they aren't sanctioned by any legal authority.

When you receive a digital certificate, you also receive instructions on how to install it on your computer. After installing the certificate, you can use it as a digital signature to sign a file.

Do it!

C-3: Discussing digital signatures

Questions and answers

1 What's a digital signature?

2 Why do you need a digital signature?

3 What's a digital certificate?

4 What are the two types of digital certificates?

5 What's a Class 2 digital certificate?

6 What's a Class 3 digital certificate?

7 What's the risk of creating your own digital certificate?

5–12 Office 2007: New Features

Topic D: Custom layouts

Explanation

PowerPoint provides default slide layouts that include master slides. You can use these default slide layouts when creating new presentations and then apply formatting to them. But if you have a specific format that you use repeatedly, you can add custom slide layouts to PowerPoint.

Custom slide layouts

To create a custom slide layout:

1 Activate the View tab.

2 Click Slide Master. The master layout displays a list of thumbnails in the task pane on the left.

3 Right-click a thumbnail in the task pane and choose Insert Layout. A new thumbnail appears for the custom slide layout inserted.

4 Right-click the new thumbnail and choose Rename Layout.

5 Enter a name for the new layout.

6 Format the slide as desired.

New PowerPoint features 5-13

Do it!

D-1: Creating custom slide layouts

Here's how	Here's why
1 Create a blank presentation	
2 Save the file as **My logo**	In the current unit folder.
3 In the Slides group, click **Layout**	
	The Layout gallery displays the default slide layouts.
Point to each of the slide layouts	A ToolTip displays each layout's name.
Click anywhere on the current slide	To close the Layout gallery.
4 Activate the View tab	You'll add a layout.
In the Presentation Views group, click **Slide Master**	To display the master layout.
Observe the slide thumbnails	The Title Slide Layout is activated by default.
5 Right-click the thumbnail and choose **Insert Layout**	To insert a custom slide layout.
Point to the new thumbnail	
	A ToolTip displays the default name, Custom Layout.

6	Right-click and choose **Rename Layout**	To open the Rename Layout dialog box.
	Edit the Layout name box to read **Logo layout**	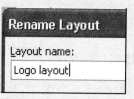
		To give the layout a more descriptive name.
	Click **Rename**	To close the dialog box.
7	Activate the Insert tab	You'll insert a picture.
	In the Illustrations group, click **Picture**	To open the Insert Picture dialog box.
	Navigate to the current unit folder	If necessary.
	Insert **LogoRotated**	Click the jpg file and then click Insert.
8	Drag the logo down and to the left	
		To align it with the other placeholders.
9	Switch to Normal view	Activate the View tab. In the Presentation Views group, click Normal.
10	Activate the Home tab	(If necessary.) You'll view the new layout.
	In the Slides group, click **Layout**	The new layout appears in the gallery.
	Point to the new layout	A ToolTip displays the name you entered for this layout.
	Click the Logo layout item	The new custom layout is applied to the current slide.
11	Update the presentation	

New PowerPoint features **5–15**

Themes

Explanation

A *theme* is a named set of colors, fonts, and effects that provides consistency in a presentation with a single click. To apply a theme, activate the Design tab. In the Themes group, choose a theme for the slides in the presentation.

Do it!

D-2: Applying themes to a presentation

Here's how	Here's why
1 Activate the Design tab	You'll apply a built-in theme to this blank presentation.
2 In the Themes group, click ⬓	(The More button is located at the bottom right of the Themes group.) To display the Themes gallery.
Move the pointer over the built-in themes in the gallery	Live preview displays the results on the presentation.
3 Select the **Trek** theme	To apply this theme to the blank presentation.
4 Update and close the presentation	

5–16 Office 2007: New Features

Unit summary: New PowerPoint features

Topic A
In this topic, you learned how to convert a bulleted list to a diagram using **SmartArt graphics**. Next, you learned how to use the **Design** and **Format contextual tabs** to change the diagram.

Topic B
In this topic, you learned about using **Office SharePoint Server 2007** with PowerPoint. Then you learned how to create a **slide library**.

Topic C
In this topic, you learned how to create a **static document** from a presentation, using the **.xps** and **.pdf** formats. Next, you learned about the collaborative review process that uses SharePoint and **Office Groove 2007**. Finally, you learned about **digital certificates** and **digital signatures**.

Topic D
In this topic, you learned how to create **custom slide layouts** and to use **themes** to format a presentation.

Independent practice activity

In this activity, you'll convert a bulleted list to a diagram. Next, you'll apply a theme to a presentation, and save the presentation in .pdf format.

1 Open Practice and save the presentation as **My practice**.

2 Convert the bulleted list to a **Text Cycle** diagram. (*Hint*: In the Paragraph group, click the Convert to SmartArt Graphic button.)

3 Activate the SmartArt Tools Design tab.

4 Use the Colors gallery to apply a color scheme of your choice. While the colors are different, your diagram should resemble the one shown in Exhibit 5-2.

5 Update the presentation.

6 Save the presentation as a XPS file in the current unit folder. (*Hint*: Use the Save As, PDF or XPS command.)

7 Observe the new XPS file when it opens in XML Viewer. When finished, close XML Viewer.

8 Close the presentation and PowerPoint 2007.

New PowerPoint features   5–17

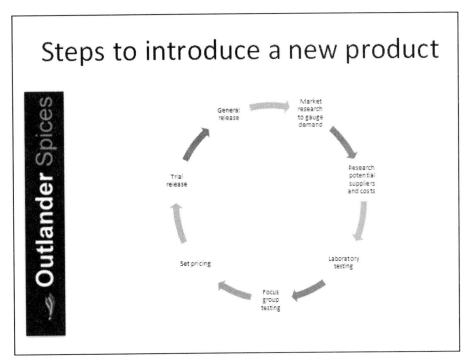

Exhibit 5-2: The slide containing the Text Cycle SmartArt graphic

5-18 Office 2007: New Features

Review questions

1 Which Ribbon group is used to convert a bulleted list to a SmartArt graphic?

   A Insert group

   B Conversion group

   C Paragraph group

   D Layouts group

2 A slide library helps prevent duplication of effort. True or false?

3 What static document formats are available in PowerPoint? (Choose all that apply.)

   A XPS

   B PDF

   C XLSM

   D DOCX

4 A SharePoint Server 2007 creates a linear workflow to manage review and feedback for a completed presentation for collaboration. True or false?

5 Which server enables team members to collaborate in real time to create a presentation?

   A SharePoint Server 2007

   B Office Groove 2007

   C Exchange Server 2007

   D Forms Server 2007

6 A digital signature is an electronic security stamp that authenticates a presentation or other Office document. True or false?

7 Which of the following are true of a theme? (Choose all that apply.)

   A A named set of colors, fonts, and effects.

   B Can't be changed, once applied.

   C Provides a consistent look to presentation elements with a single-click.

   D Can be previewed with Live Preview.

Unit 6

New Outlook features

Unit time: 60 minutes

Complete this unit, and you'll know how to:

A Use Instant Search to search for specific Outlook items, assign items to color categories, preview attachments, and subscribe to RSS feeds.

B Use the To-Do Bar to track tasks and other items, and flag Outlook items for follow up.

C Discuss the benefits of publishing online calendars, send calendar snapshots, create custom electronic business cards, and discuss the benefits of using Microsoft Exchange Server.

Topic A: Content management tools

Explanation

Outlook 2007 provides content management tools that help you search for content and categorize items using color. You can preview attachments created in other Office applications without actually opening them, and you can use Outlook 2007 to subscribe to RSS feeds.

Instant Search

You can use *Instant Search* and advanced Instant Search features to search for Outlook items, such as messages, contacts, appointments, meeting requests, and tasks, based on a specific word or phrase.

Performing a simple Instant Search

As shown in Exhibit 6-1, Instant Search appears at the top of the Folder pane. To perform a simple search:

1 In the text box, type a keyword or phrase. As you type, Outlook searches for and highlights the letters you're typing. Items containing the search phrase appear in the Folder Contents list.

2 After the search is completed, click the Clear Search button to clear the search and display all the folder items in the Folder Contents list.

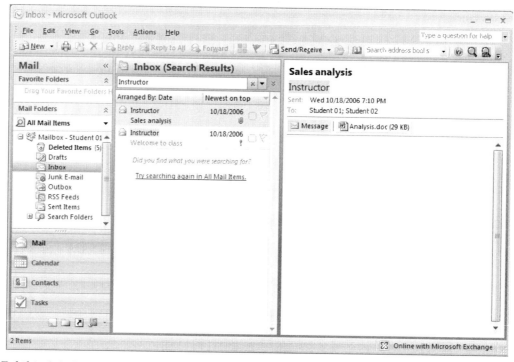

Exhibit 6-1: Instant Search results in Outlook 2007

New Outlook features   **6–3**

Performing an advanced Instant Search

To perform an advanced Instant Search, click the down-arrow to the right of the text box to expand Instant Search. For messages, four default criteria are selected: From, Body, Subject, and To. To start a search, enter a keyword or phrase in one or more of the criteria text boxes. To add a criterion, click Add Criterion and choose the criterion you want to use. To remove a criterion, click it and choose Remove Criterion.

Do it!

A-1: Using Instant Search

Here's how	Here's why
1 Click **Start** and choose **All Programs, Microsoft Office, Microsoft Office Outlook 2007**	To start Microsoft Outlook.
2 Observe the Navigation Pane	It displays the active pane, and it contains buttons, such as Mail, Contacts, and Tasks, that you can use to access other panes and folders in Outlook.
3 Activate your Inbox	(If necessary.) You'll search for all messages received from your instructor.
4 Observe the Folder pane	Notice Instant Search is located at the top of the Folder pane. By default, Outlook searches for messages in the selected folder.
5 In the text box, enter **Instructor**	Inbox / Instructor To search for messages from your instructor. As shown in Exhibit 6-1, search results display in the Folder pane.
6 On the Find bar, click the Clear Search button	(At the right end of the Find bar.) To clear the search and display all the messages in the Folder Contents list.
7 Click as shown	Newest on top / Expand the Query Builder To expand the Query Builder. Instant Search expands to show four default criteria you can use to narrow your search.

8	In the From box, enter **Instructor**	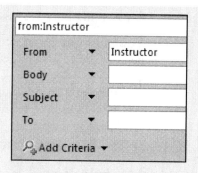
		To display the three messages from your Instructor in the Folder Contents list.
9	Click the arrow next to Body	To display the criteria choices.
	Choose **Remove**	To remove Body as one of the criteria.
10	Remove the To criterion	Click the arrow next to To and choose Remove.
11	In the Subject box, enter **Urgent**	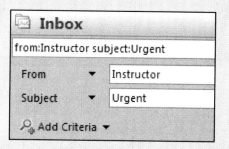
		To locate the message from your instructor with the subject Urgent.
12	Click **Clear**	
13	Click **Add Criteria**	
	Choose **Body**	To add the Body criterion back as a search criteria.
14	Add the To criterion back as a search criteria	
15	Collapse Instant Search	Click the up-arrow button.

Color categories

Explanation

You can group related items by assigning them a color category. *Color categories* can be assigned to messages, contacts, appointments, or other Outlook items.

To categorize an item:

1. Open the message or other item.
2. In the tab, click Categorize.
3. Choose a category or click All Categories to open the Color Categories dialog box. You can use the buttons on the right side to create new color categories, rename or delete existing ones, or apply different colors.
4. Click OK.

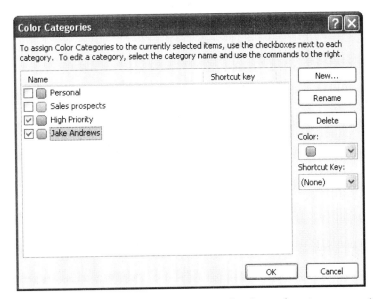

Exhibit 6-2: The Color Categories dialog box, showing customized categories

6–6 Office 2007: New Features

Do it!

A-2: Organizing content by using Color Categories

Here's how	Here's why
1 In the Navigation pane, click **Calendar**	To display the calendar in the center pane.
2 Double-click a time on the calendar	To begin a new appointment. The appointment item opens.
In the Subject line, enter **Presentation to the board**	To name this appointment.
3 In the Options group, click **Categorize**	

Choose **All Categories...**	To open the Color Categories dialog box.
4 Double-click the Red Category and then click **Rename**	You'll change the default category name.
Edit the name to read **High Priority**	

5 Change the name of the Blue Category to **Personal**	Click Blue Category, then click Rename. Edit the name to read Personal.
Change the name of the Green Category to **Sales prospects**	
6 Click **New**	The Add New Category dialog box appears.
Edit the name to read **Jake Andrews**	

	The name of the chairman of Outlander Spices.
In the Color list, select **Maroon**	
Click **OK**	To add the new category and close the dialog box. By default, Outlook checks this category.

7	Select the Orange Category and then click **Delete**	To delete this category. A Microsoft Office Outlook window prompts you to confirm the deletion.
	Click **Yes**	To confirm the deletion.
	Delete the Purple and Yellow categories	Compare your Color Categories dialog box to the one shown in Exhibit 6-2.
8	Click **OK**	To close the Color Categories dialog box and assign this calendar appointment to the High Priority and Jake Andrews categories.
9	Observe the appointment item window	 The category bar appears above the Subject box. Jake Andrews category bar is maroon, and the High Priority bar is red.
	Save and close the appointment	
10	In the calendar window, locate the new appointment	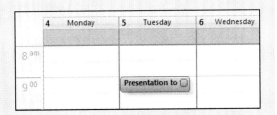 (Switch to Week view, if necessary.) The appointment appears on the calendar, shaded maroon. The red square indicates the High Priority category.
11	Activate the Mail tab	
	In the Standard toolbar, click	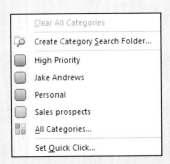 Clicking the Categorize button displays the same categories you created.
	Press ESC	To close the menu without making a selection.

Preview attachments

Explanation

When you receive an e-mail that includes an attached file, you can preview the file in Outlook 2007 without actually opening it.

Previewing an attachment is fast and convenient. You don't have to wait for the document's application to launch, and then navigate multiple windows on your desktop. The attachment displays within the Outlook message.

To preview an Office file, that file's application must be installed on your PC. For example, to preview an Excel worksheet in Outlook, Excel must be installed. Outlook can preview many other file formats, such as HTML, image, or text files, without actually opening them.

To preview an attachment:

1 Open the e-mail that contains the attachment.
2 In the Reading pane, click the attachment icon. A message appears in the Reading Pane.
3 Click Preview File. Outlook displays the file in the Reading Pane.
4 To return to the text of the e-mail, click Message.

Do it!

A-3: Previewing an attachment

Here's how	Here's why
1 Work with a partner and send the message with an attachment, as shown	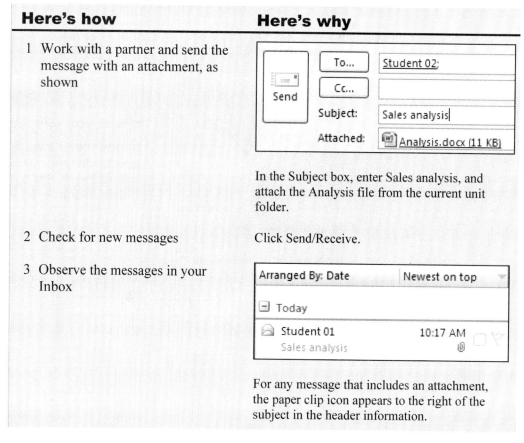 In the Subject box, enter Sales analysis, and attach the Analysis file from the current unit folder.
2 Check for new messages	Click Send/Receive.
3 Observe the messages in your Inbox	For any message that includes an attachment, the paper clip icon appears to the right of the subject in the header information.

4 Select a message with an attachment

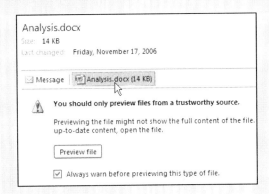

To display the contents of the message in the Reading Pane. Near the top of the pane, a Message button and the attachment name and size display.

5 In the Reading Pane, click the attachment file name

The Reading Pane now displays details about the file attachment: file name, size, author, and the last changed date. In the middle of the pane, Outlook displays a warning message that you should preview files only from a trustworthy source.

   Click **Preview File**

To preview the attachment in the Reading Pane. If you don't have Word installed, then you can't preview the file.

6 Click **Message**

To close the attachment preview and display the message text again.

RSS feeds

Explanation

You can use Outlook 2007 to subscribe to *RSS* (Really Simple Syndication) feeds. RSS feeds deliver summaries of updates to popular Web sites. By clicking the summary, you can view the full content.

You can use the following methods to add RSS feeds to your Outlook mail. The first method is the easiest.

1. In Outlook, click RSS Feeds. An explanation of RSS feeds appears in the Reading pane.
2. Scroll down to view links to a variety of RSS feeds.
3. Click the desired RSS feed. For example, MSDN articles focusing on Office. You're prompted to add the feed to your Outlook.
4. Click Yes to add the feed to Outlook.
5. Click Yes to accept the message about accepting information from secure sites.
6. Once the RSS feed has been added, your screen should resemble the one shown in Exhibit 6-3.

You can also use the Options dialog box to subscribe to an RSS feed:

1. Choose Tools, Options to open the Options dialog box.
2. Activate the Mail Setup tab.
3. Click E-mail Accounts to open the Account Settings dialog box.
4. Activate the RSS Feeds tab.
5. Click New. The New RSS Feed dialog box appears.
6. Enter the URL (Web address) of the RSS feed and click Add.
7. Click Close, then click OK.

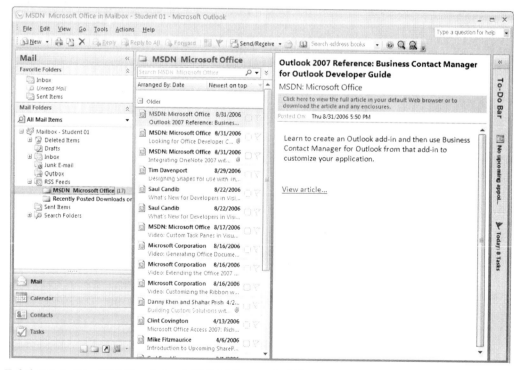

Exhibit 6-3: The RSS Feeds for MSDN Microsoft Office

New Outlook features **6–11**

Do it! **A-4: Subscribing to RSS feeds**

Here's how	Here's why
1 Activate Mail	If necessary.
Under Mail Folders, click **RSS Feeds**	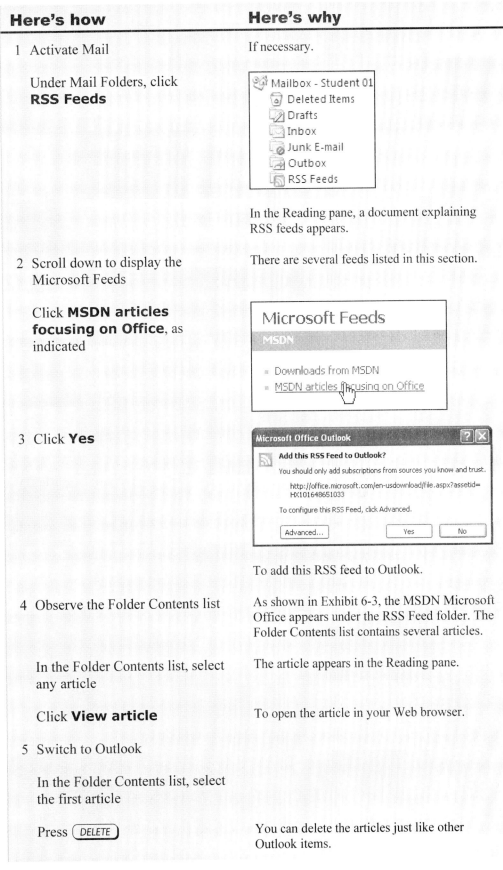
	In the Reading pane, a document explaining RSS feeds appears.
2 Scroll down to display the Microsoft Feeds	There are several feeds listed in this section.
Click **MSDN articles focusing on Office**, as indicated	
3 Click **Yes**	
	To add this RSS feed to Outlook.
4 Observe the Folder Contents list	As shown in Exhibit 6-3, the MSDN Microsoft Office appears under the RSS Feed folder. The Folder Contents list contains several articles.
In the Folder Contents list, select any article	The article appears in the Reading pane.
Click **View article**	To open the article in your Web browser.
5 Switch to Outlook	
In the Folder Contents list, select the first article	
Press (DELETE)	You can delete the articles just like other Outlook items.

6 Right-click any RSS feed

To display the shortcut menu for the RSS feed item.

Choose **Download Content**, **Download article**

To download the article to Outlook.

In the Reading Pane, click **Full article.htm**

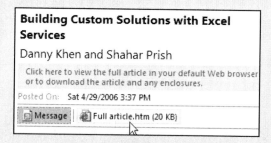

To view the article in the Reading pane. However, if you don't have the required previewer, clicking this link opens the article in a Web browser window.

7 Close the browser window

Topic B: The To-Do Bar

Explanation

Outlook's To-Do Bar displays messages, appointments, and meetings that you've flagged for follow-up. When you create a task, it's automatically flagged for follow-up.

To-Do Bar

The To-Do Bar appears on the right side of the Outlook window. The three states of the To-Do Bar are Off (default for Mail folder), Minimized, and Normal. To display the To-Do Bar in Normal view, you can click the Normal view button or choose View, To-Do Bar, Normal. You can also press Alt+F2 to toggle through the To-Do Bar views.

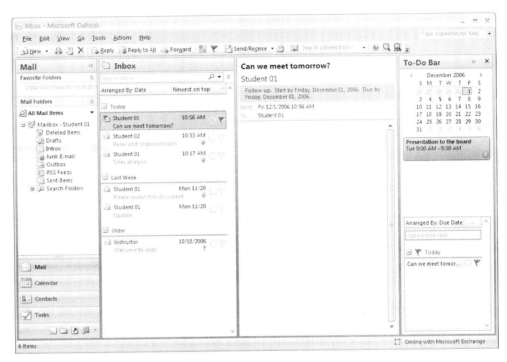

Exhibit 6-4: The To-Do Bar in Normal view

Flagging an item for follow-up

To add an item, such as a message, to the To-Do Bar, you flag it for follow-up. This attaches a flag symbol to the message and copies it to the To-Do Bar. The flag serves as a visual reminder that the item requires further attention. You can also send a flagged message to others, so that they know that action is required.

To flag a message, right-click the flag column to the right of the message and select a flag. A flagged message appears in the To-Do Bar, in Tasks, and in the Daily Task list in Calendar.

Completed messages

After you follow up on a flagged message, you can open the Flag menu again and choose Mark Complete. The flag changes to a check mark, and the message is removed from the To-Do Bar.

6–14   Office 2007: New Features

Do it!

B-1:   Flagging a message

Here's how	Here's why
1 Open the Inbox	
2 Choose **View**, **To-Do Bar**, **Normal**	To display the To-Do Bar in Normal view, as shown in Exhibit 6-4.
3 Create a new message	Address the message to your e-mail partner.
Enter a subject of **Can we meet tomorrow?**	You'll create a message that a recipient can use to set up an appointment.
In the message area, type **Please let me know when you'll be available tomorrow.**	
4 In the Options group, click **Follow Up**	
Choose **Today**	
5 Observe the InfoBar	The InfoBar displays the flag for follow-up information.
6 Send the message	Click Send.
7 Observe the new message from your partner	The message asking you to meet tomorrow appears flagged, as shown in Exhibit 6-4.

Using the To-Do Bar

Explanation

As shown in Exhibit 6-5, the four areas of the To-Do Bar include:
- Date Navigator: A small calendar interface to help you find an upcoming date.
- Appointments: Your scheduled appointments.
- Task Input panel: A text entry area for typing in your tasks.
- Task List: Your list of things to do.

Exhibit 6-5: To-Do Bar elements

Creating tasks

To create a task, type the task into the Task Input Panel on the To-Do Bar. You can also create a task by choosing File, New, Task, or by clicking the New button while in the Tasks pane.

By default, a task entered in the Task Input Panel is given a due date and start date of today. You can change this by double-clicking the task to edit its settings.

6–16 Office 2007: New Features

Do it!

B-2: Adding a new task to the To-Do Bar

Here's how	Here's why
1 Activate the Calendar	You'll create a new task for tomorrow. By default, the To-Do Bar is displayed in Normal view.
Switch to Day view	If necessary.
Activate the To-Do Bar	(If necessary.) Choose View, To-Do Bar, Normal.
2 In the To-Do Bar's Date Navigator, select tomorrow's date	You'll create a new task for tomorrow. The Calendar pane displays tomorrow's appointments
3 In the To-Do Bar, point to the Task Input panel, as indicated	Arranged By: Due Date ▲ ▲ Type a new task You can click here to enter a new task.
In the Task Input panel, type **Outlook 2007 Class**	Arranged By: Due Date ▲ ▲ Outlook 2007 Class
Press (↵ ENTER)	The task appears on the To-Do Bar, as shown in Exhibit 6-5, and in the Tasks pane at the bottom of the Calendar folder.
4 In the Navigation pane, click **Mail**	To navigate away from the Calendar.
5 On the To-Do Bar, right-click the Outlook Class task	To display the task shortcut menu.
Choose **Delete**	To delete the task from your Task list.
6 In the To-Do Bar title bar, click the Minimize button, as shown	To-Do Bar » × ◄ Minimize the To-Do Bar To minimize the To-Do Bar.
7 Expand the To-Do Bar	« Expand the To-Do Bar Click the Expand button to return the To-Do Bar to Normal view.

New Outlook features   **6–17**

Topic C: Shared content

Explanation

Outlook 2007 provides features that make it easier to share information with co-workers in a team environment. You can publish your personal calendar online for others to see, or you can e-mail just a snapshot of a specific range of dates. You can also create an electronic business card to send others your personal information. And Microsoft Exchange makes it both easier and more secure to share information online.

Publishing calendars

When all of your team members are on the same network, it's easy to give them access to your Outlook calendar so that they can send meeting requests. Outlook 2007 makes it easy to share your calendar outside of your network, by publishing your calendar online.

You can use Outlook to create an *iCal* (Internet Calendar) file, and then publish that file to Microsoft Office Online. *Microsoft Office Online* is a Microsoft Web site that provides tools and services to Office users. Using Microsoft Passport credentials, you can restrict access to the file to authorized users. Users who are granted access to your calendar can use it to send and respond to meeting requests.

Do it!

C-1: Discussing Internet calendar publishing

Questions and answers
1   What's an Internet calendar?
2   How are Internet calendars created?
3   What's Microsoft Office Online?
4   What's the benefit of publishing your personal calendar to Microsoft Office Online?
5   What security is available to restrict access to your calendar after it's published and available online?

Calendar snapshots

Explanation

You can e-mail a specific date range in your calendar. The resulting *snapshot* of a specific time period isn't interactive—the person receiving it can't use it to send meeting requests. But they can use it to determine when you are available, and send requests based on that.

You can control the level of detail that is sent. Your snapshot can show only your availability, or it can include the details of your meetings and appointments.

To send a calendar snapshot:

1 Activate the Calendar.
2 In the Navigation Pane, click Send Calendar via E-mail. The Send a Calendar via E-Mail dialog box appears, as shown in Exhibit 6-6.
3 If you keep more than one calendar, select one in the Calendar list.
4 In the Date Range list, select a preconfigured date range, such as Next 7 days, or select Specific dates to display the Start and End date fields.
5 In the Detail list, select the level of detail that you want to send regarding your appointments.
6 Click OK.

The Advanced button displays two options that apply to detail levels greater than Availability Only. If you elect to send Limited details or Full details, you can choose to include details for items that are marked private. If you elect to send Full details, you can elect to include any attachments that are present for calendar items.

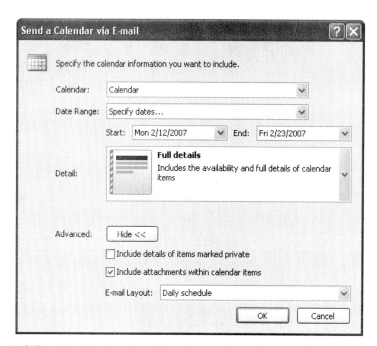

Exhibit 6-6: The Send a Calendar via E-mail dialog box

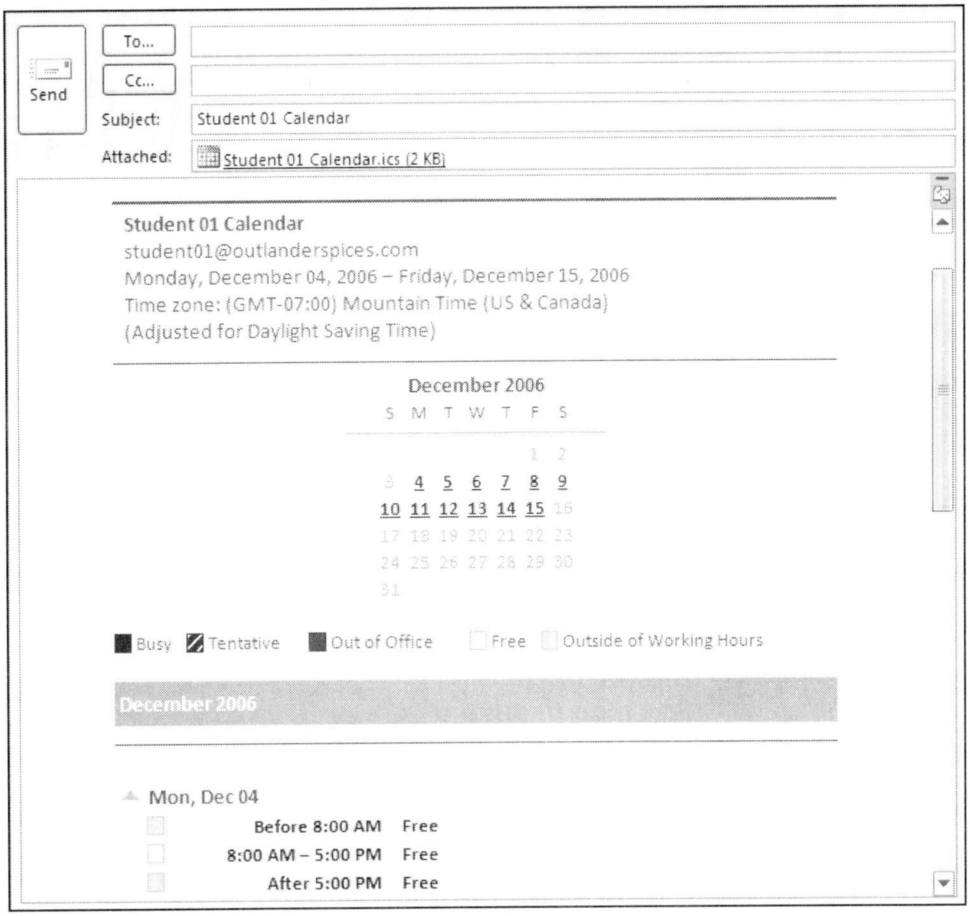

New Outlook features **6–19**

Exhibit 6-7: A sample of a calendar snapshot being sent via e-mail

Do it!

C-2: Creating calendar snapshots

Here's how	Here's why
1 In the Navigation pane, click Calendar	To activate the Calendar pane and display the Calendar folder to the right of the Navigation Pane.
2 In the Navigation Pane, click **Send a Calendar via E-mail...**	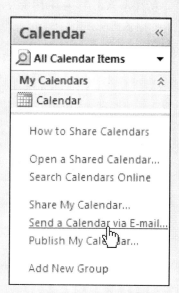 Outlook begins a new message. The Send a Calendar via E-mail dialog box appears.
3 In the Date Range list, select **Specify dates**	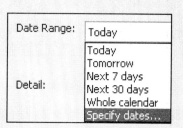
Using the Start and End boxes, select any two-week period in the future	
In the Detail list, select **Full details**	To include details about your meetings and appointments in the snapshot.
4 Under Advanced, click **Show**	To display the Advanced options.
5 Verify that Include details of items marked private is clear	This is a business e-mail, so you won't include personal information.
Check **Include attachments with calendar items**	To allow your correspondent to open and read any documentation or other files attached to your appointments and meetings. Compare your dialog box to he one shown in Exhibit 6-6.

6	Click **OK**	To close the dialog box.
7	Observe the body of the e-mail message	The calendar snapshot has been inserted into the body of the e-mail message. It's also included as an attachment, as shown in Exhibit 6-7.
8	Address the e-mail to your partner and send it	
9	Switch to Mail	If necessary.
	Observe your partner's calendar in the Reading pane	

In the Reading pane, the calendar that was sent is visible. If you've been given rights to your partner's calendar, you can click Open this calendar at the top of the Reading pane.

Electronic business cards

Explanation

You give business cards to your colleagues and other business contacts to introduce yourself and to provide them with your contact information. With Outlook 2007, you can create electronic business cards and e-mail them to others.

An *electronic business card* is a small file that looks like a paper business card when displayed in Outlook, as shown in Exhibit 6-8. You can insert logos or other graphics on the card, select background and text colors, and enter your personal information and contact data. When you mail it to colleagues, each of them can save your electronic business card in their Contacts folder in Outlook.

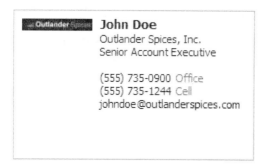

Exhibit 6-8: An electronic business card for John Doe

Create an electronic business card

To create a custom electronic business card:

1 On the toolbar, click the arrow beside New and choose Contact. The Contact dialog box appears.

2 If you wish to add a picture, then, in the Options group, click the arrow beneath Picture and choose Add Picture. The Add Contact Picture dialog box appears.

3 Navigate to the desired picture and click OK.

4 Complete the Full Name field and other text fields that you want to include on the electronic business card. As you complete each field, it displays on the Business Card at the bottom left of the dialog box.

5 In the Options group, click Business Card. The Edit Business Card dialog box appears.

6 Use the Edit Business Card dialog box to configure the card. You can add, delete, and change the order of text fields. You can change the card layout and background, and change the color, font, and alignment of text fields.

7 Click OK to close the Edit Business Card dialog box.

8 In the Actions group, click Save & Close.

9 Begin an e-mail message.

10 In the Actions group, click Save & Close.

New Outlook features 6-23

Exhibit 6-9: The Edit Business Card dialog box

6–24 Office 2007: New Features

Do it!

C-3: Creating an electronic business card

Here's how	Here's why
1 Click the arrow beside New and choose **Contact**	(The New button is on the toolbar.) A new Contact window appears. You'll create an electronic business card for yourself. The Contact tab is activated by default.
2 In the Options group, click **Picture** and select **Add picture...**	
	The Add Contact Picture dialog box appears.
From the current unit folder, add **logo**	To add the Outlander Spices logo at the top of the electronic business card.
3 In the Full Name box, enter your name	
In the Company box, enter **Outlander Spices, Inc.**	To add the company name to the business card.
In the Job title box, enter **Senior Account Executive**	To add a title to the business card.
4 In the E-mail box enter an e-mail address in the following format	
Your_name@outlanderspices.com	
5 Under Phone numbers, in the Business box, enter **555 735 0900**	To add an office phone numbers to the business card. Outlook automatically adds parentheses around the area code and hyphenates the number.
In the Mobile box, enter **555 735 1244**	To enter a cell phone number.
6 In the Options group, click **Business Card**	To open the Edit Business Card dialog box.

7 Under Fields, select **Business Phone**

Fields
Full Name
Company
Job Title
  Blank Line
Business Phone
Mobile Phone

Edit the Label box to read **Office**

(555) 735-0900

Label: Office

To change the label for this line.

Edit the Label field for Mobile Phone to read **Cell**

(Under Fields, select Mobile Phone and enter Cell in the Label field.) Compare your screen to the one shown in Exhibit 6-9.

Click **OK**

To close the dialog box.

8 In the Actions group, click **Save & Close**

To save the electronic business card and close the window.

Attach an electronic business card as stationery

Explanation

You can designate any electronic business card as your default card. This makes it easy to attach the card to outgoing e-mail messages—either automatically or on a per-message basis. To designate a default card:

1 Begin a new Mail Message.
2 In the Include group, click the arrow beside Signature and choose Signatures. The Signature and Stationery dialog box appears.
3 Click New. The New Signature dialog box appears.
4 Enter a name for this card and click OK.
5 Under Edit signature, click Business Card. The Insert Business Card dialog box appears.
6 Double-click the electronic business card you created for yourself to enter it in the Signatures and Stationery dialog box.
7 Under Choose default signature, in the New messages list, select the name of the business card to attach the card automatically to every outgoing e-mail message.
8 Click OK to close the Signatures and Stationery dialog box.

To attach a business card while working on an outgoing message, click the arrow beside Signatures and choose the business card by name.

Exhibit 6-10: A new e-mail message with an attached business card

New Outlook features **6–27**

Do it!

C-4: Inserting and sending a business card

Here's how	Here's why
1 Create a new e-mail message	You'll create a signature that uses this electronic business card.
2 In the Include group, click **Business Card**	To display a list of business cards.
Select **Other Business Cards...**	To open the Insert Business Card dialog box.
Select the business card you created for yourself	
Click **OK**	As shown in Exhibit 6-10, your electronic business card is inserted in the body of the e-mail message and is included as an attachment in the form of a .vcf file.
3 Close the message without saving or sending it	

6–28 Office 2007: New Features

Exchange Server

Explanation

Exchange Server is an enterprise-level application that complements Outlook. For Office 2007, Exchange Server 2003 provides a number of services and features that extend the functionality of Outlook.

Security

To help reduce junk mail, Exchange Server performs a prescreening of inbound mail before it's delivered to your Outlook inbox. To help guard against phishing scams and other malicious e-mail, Exchange Server can disable URLs or other links that it deems suspicious.

Managed folders

Exchange Server can perform folder maintenance operations to achieve regulatory compliance or to adhere to internal organizational policies. Exchange Server can manage folder retention, archiving, and deletion according to each organization's needs.

Exchange Server can also grant read and/or write permissions to your Outlook folders to specific co-workers.

Scheduling

The scheduling assistant included in Exchange Server can simplify the task of scheduling meetings with a large, scattered group. For example, the scheduling assistant can examine a group's calendars and locations and suggest the best time and place for a meeting.

When the details of a meeting change, Exchange Server can send each attendee an e-mail message notifying them of the change. The attendees don't receive a new invitation that they have to accept. The exception to this is meeting time: if that changes, then new invitations are sent out.

Unified Messaging

Unified Messaging can send telephone voicemail messages and faxes that you receive directly to your Outlook inbox. The voicemail messages play as sound files over your computer's speakers, and the faxes display on your screen. This can be especially useful when traveling, because you can now pick up all messages in one place.

Out of office

Exchange Server can deliver one out-of-office message to people within your organization and a different one to external contacts. These messages can be configured to begin and end at specific times.

Do it!

C-5: Discussing Exchange Server collaboration

Questions and answers

1 What does Microsoft Exchange do to protect against junk e-mail?

2 What features does Microsoft Exchange provide for managed folders?

3 What scheduling features are included?

4 What's Unified Messaging?

5 What out-of-office features does Microsoft Exchange provide?

6–30 Office 2007: New Features

Unit summary: New Outlook features

Topic A

In this topic, you used **Instant Search** to scan your e-mail messages or other Outlook items for specific content. Then, you assigned **color categories** to Outlook items and customized the colors. Next, you learned how to **preview files** in the Reading pane of a message. Finally, you discussed subscribing to **RSS feeds** from within Outlook 2007.

Topic B

In this topic, you learned how to add items to the **To-Do Bar**. You **flagged** an item for follow-up and added **tasks.** You also experimented with the three ways to view the To-Do Bar.

Topic C

In this topic, you learned about the benefits of publishing your **calendar online**. You discussed creating **calendar snapshots** and created **custom electronic business cards**. Finally, you learned about the benefits of using **Microsoft Exchange Server** to extend the functionality of Outlook 2007.

Independent practice activity

In this activity, you'll flag an e-mail message for follow-up and add a task. Then you'll create an electronic business card, and subscribe to an RSS feed.

1 Flag an e-mail message to be followed up next week. When you're done, close the message without saving it. (*Hint*: In the Options group, click Follow Up.)

2 Add a task for next week. (*Hint*: Choose View, To-Do Bar, Normal. Use the To-Do Bar's Date Navigator to select a date next week. In the Task Input pane, enter a name for the task and press Enter.)

3 Use the To-Do Bar to open and edit the task you scheduled. Save and close the task, then turn off the To-Do Bar.

4 Create an e-mail message that includes a snapshot of your calendar for tomorrow. (*Hint*: Click Send a Calendar via e-Mail.)

5 Close Microsoft Office Outlook 2007.

Review questions

1 You can reduce the number of items returned by an Instant Search by Using advanced Instant Search and specifying sender, date, subject, or other criteria. True or false?

2 Which of the following is true about color categories? (Choose all that apply.)

A Can be assigned to messages.

B Can be renamed with more personal names.

C Can be deleted if the color is never used.

D Is available only for e-mail messages.

New Outlook features   **6–31**

3 What's the requirement for previewing an attached file in the Reading pane?

    A A version of the attached file must reside on your computer.

    B XML Viewer must be installed on your computer.

    C SharePoint Server 2007 must be set up and running.

    D The source application must be installed on your computer.

4 What does the acronym RSS represent?

    A Real-time Subscription Service

    B Really Simple Subscriptions

    C Really Simple Syndication

    D Real-time Simple Subscriptions

5 Flagging an Outlook item serves as a reminder to follow up on that item. True or false?

6 You can't share your appointment calendar with users who aren't on your network. True or false?

7 Which of the following is true of a calendar snapshot? (Choose all that apply.)

    A A calendar snapshot is a specific date range from your personal calendar.

    B You can e-mail a calendar snapshot to someone.

    C A calendar snapshot is interactive.

    D Calendar snapshots resemble the Date Navigator.

8 An electronic business card is the online equivalent of a paper business card that you might hand to a colleague or business contact. True or false?

Office 2007: New Features

Unit 7
New Access features

Unit time: 45 minutes

Complete this unit, and you'll know how to:

A Display open items as tabbed documents in the Access window, use Lookup fields and Attachment fields, and append or modify data by using e-mail.

B Modify reports in Layout view; and sort, filter, and group reports.

Topic A: Data features

Explanation

Access 2007 uses tabbed items to make it easier to manage multiple open tables, queries, or reports. You can use a Lookup Field to choose a field entry in a table from a list. The Attachment data type supports attaching documents or other files to fields in a database. Access 2007 can accept and automatically process e-mail messages that include data to be added or modified in a table.

The document window

Earlier versions of Access used floating windows to display multiple open items. This format is still available, but the default format for Access 2007 displays open items as tabbed documents, as shown in Exhibit 7-1.

However, if you open a database that was created with a previous version of Access, you might need to change the window option setting to display the tabbed documents. To do so:

1. Click the Office Button and click Access Options to open the Access Options dialog box.
2. From the category list, select Current Database.
3. Under Application Options, select Tabbed Documents for the Document Window Option setting.
4. Check Display Document Tabs.
5. Click OK.

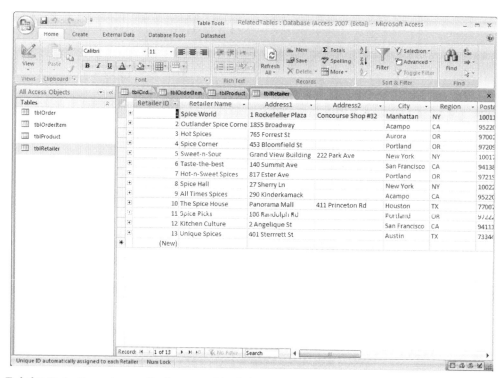

Exhibit 7-1: Open items display as tabbed documents

New Access features   **7–3**

Do it!

A-1: Using the document window

Here's how	Here's why
1 Open Microsoft Office Access 2007	Click Start and choose All Programs, Microsoft Office, Microsoft Office Access 2007.
2 Open RelatedTables	From the current unit folder.
In the Read-Only Warning, click **Save As**	(If necessary.) A Save As box appears.
Save the database as MyRelatedTables	In the current unit folder.
3 In the Security Warning, click **Options**	A Microsoft Security Options dialog box appears.
Select **Enable this Content** and click **OK**	To close the Security Options dialog box.
4 Open tblOrder	The table opens in a window. This database was saved in the overlapping windows format used by older versions of Access.
5 Open tblRetailer	This table also opens in a separate window. This new window is superimposed over the tblOrder window, completely obscuring it. To see the first table's window, you have to drag this window.
Close tblOrder and tblRetailer	You'll convert this database file to use the Access 2007 document window style.
6 Open the Access Options dialog box	Click the Office Button, then choose Access Options.
Select the **Current Database** category	To see startup options for the current database.

7	Under Document Window Options, select **Tabbed Documents**	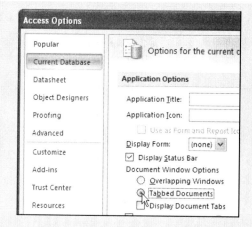
	Check **Display Document Tabs**	
		This is the new document window option. It's the default for new databases.
	Click **OK**	To close the dialog box.
	Click **OK** again	To accept the message.
8	Close the database	You must close and reopen the database to see the changes you made.
9	Open MyRelatedTables	
	In the Security Warning, enable the content	Click Options, and select Enable this Content, and click OK.
	Open all of the tables in the database	The document window displays the four open tables as a series of tabbed windows, as shown in Exhibit 7-1.
10	Click the tblOrder tab	To display the tblOrder table.
	Activate the other table tabs	To view the other open tables.
11	Right-click the tblOrder tab	
	Choose **Close**	To close the tblOrder tab.
12	Close tblProduct and tblRetailer	You'll use tblOrderItem in the next activity.

Lookup fields

Explanation

A *Lookup field* lists values from another field in the same or another table, or from a user-defined list. Rather than typing in data, the Lookup field provides a dropdown list from which you can select a value. The Lookup Wizard helps you create a Lookup field, which you can later modify.

Lookup fields can make data entry easier and ensure that entered data is valid. For instance, the product field in an invoice table could list only the values of the product name column in the product table. This saves typing and ensures that only valid products are placed in the invoice table. A Lookup field can also display a list of user-defined values, instead of a column from a table or query. The list that a Lookup field displays is called a *Lookup list*.

Lookup lists

You can create a Lookup list in the Design view of a table. The Lookup list extracts a list of values from a field in another table. You need to delete any relationships between the tables before creating a Lookup field. The reason for this is that you can't change the data type of a field if the table is related to another table.

7–6 Office 2007: New Features

Do it!

A-2: Preparing to use the Lookup wizard

Here's how	Here's why
1 Observe tblOrderItem	The Product column contains the Product IDs for the company's products. The details about each product are stored in the tblProduct table. To select a product name from a Lookup list, you'll make the Product column a Lookup field, instead of typing the product ID.
2 On the Status bar, click the Design View button	To switch to Design view.
Click the Data Type column of strItemProductID	You'll make this field a Lookup field.
From the Data Type list, select **Lookup Wizard...**	A warning message indicates that you can't change the data type, as the field is a part of one or more relationships.
Click **OK**	To close the message box.
3 Close tblOrderItem	A message box asks if you want to save changes to the table design.
Click **No**	To close the table without saving any changes.
4 Activate the Database Tools tab	(In the Ribbon.) You'll delete the relationship between tblOrderItem and tblProduct.
In the Show/Hide group, click **Relationships**	To open the Relationships window.

In the Design View table:

Field Name	Data Type
lngItemID	AutoNumber
lngItemOrdID	Number
strItemProductID	Text
sngItemQuantity	Number

Show/Hide group:
- Relationships
- Property Sheet
- Object Dependencies
- ✓ Message Bar

5 Delete the relationship between tblOrderItem and tblProduct

   Click **Yes**

   Close the Relationships window

In the Relationships window, select the relationship between tblOrderItem and tblProduct and press Delete.

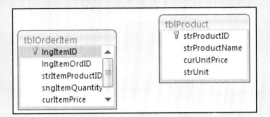

To confirm the deletion of the relationship between the two tables.

7–8 Office 2007: New Features

Creating a Lookup list

Explanation

To create a Lookup list that looks up values in a table or query:

1 Delete any relationship between the table where you want to create a Lookup field and the table containing the Lookup data.

2 In Design view, open the table in which you want to create the Lookup field.

3 Click in the Data Type column of the field in which you want to create the list. A dropdown arrow appears.

4 Click the dropdown arrow and select Lookup Wizard to start the wizard.

5 Select the first option to specify that you want to look up the values in a table or a query, and then click Next.

6 Under View, select the desired option.

7 From the list, select an object, and then click Next.

8 From the Available Fields list, select the desired field. Click Add to add the field to the Selected Fields list, and then click Next.

9 Select the field based on which the list should be sorted, and then click Next. The wizard displays a column of values for the previously specified field.

10 Extend the column width to fit all the values in the column, if necessary, and then click Next.

11 Enter a label for the Lookup field, and then click Finish. A message box prompts you to save the table.

12 Click Yes to save the table and create the Lookup list in the field.

13 Set the relationships between the related fields.

Order Detail	Order ID	Product	Quantity	Price Paid
40	19	Basil Leaf (Grou	100	$1.45
41	19	Product Nan	100	$1.25
42	20	Cassia	50	$1.00
43	20	Catnip Leaf	50	$3.50
45	22	Celery Seed	80	$1.50
46	22	Celery Seed	90	$2.00
47	22	Chamomile	200	$1.49
48	23	Chili Pepper	250	$2.00
49	23	Chinese Star	250	$4.25
51	25	Chinese Star	50	$2.75
52	25	Chives	75	$2.29
53	25	Cilantro Flak	85	$1.89
54	26	De Arbol Pe	300	$4.25
55	26	De Arbol Pe	300	$5.50
56	26	Annatto See	400	$3.50
57	26	Cinnamon G	100	$1.00
58	26	Cinnamon (c	500	$2.00
59	27	Asafoetida F	200	$3.00
60	27	Anise Seeds	250	$1.23
61	28	Basil Leaf (V	50	$1.23
62	28	Carob Pods	25	$5.50
63	28	Carob Powd	25	$3.00
64	27	Basil Leaf (G	170	$1.25
65	5	Caraway See	100	$1.25
66	27	Cinnamon G		

Record: 59 of 59   No Filter   Search

Exhibit 7-2: A Lookup list

Do it!

A-3: Creating a Lookup list field

Here's how	Here's why
1 Open tblOrderItem in Design view	In the Tables list, right-click tblOrderItem and choose Design view.
Click in the Data Type column of strItemProductID	

Field Name	Data Type
lngItemID	AutoNumber
lngItemOrdID	Number
strItemProductID	Text
sngItemQuantity	Number

You'll change the data type of the field.

From the Data Type list, select **Lookup Wizard...**

Text
Text
Memo
Number
Date/Time
Currency
AutoNumber
Yes/No
OLE Object
Hyperlink
Attachment
Lookup Wizard...

To start the Lookup Wizard.

2 Verify that the first option is selected

⊙ I want the lookup column to look up the values in a table or query.

○ I will type in the values that I want.

You'll create a Lookup list based on field values in a table.

Click **Next**

3 Under View, verify that Tables is selected

View
⊙ Tables   ○ Queries   ○ Both

From the list, select **Table: tblProduct**

Table: tblOrder
Table: tblProduct
Table: tblRetailer

You'll create a Lookup list based on field values in this table.

Click **Next**

This dialog box shows a list of fields in the table you selected. Here, you can specify the fields on which to base the Lookup list.

7–10 Office 2007: New Features

4 From the Available Fields list, select **strProductName**	You'll create a lookup field based on this field.
Click [>]	To add strProductName to the Selected Fields list.
Click **Next**	The wizard displays options for sorting the list.
5 Click **Next**	The list of products appears in the Product Name column. You can resize the column width, if necessary.
6 Click **Next**	You'll use strItemProductID as the label.
7 Click **Finish**	A message box prompts you to save the table.
Click **Yes**	To save the table and create the Lookup field.
8 Close the table	
9 Open the Relationships window	Activate the Database Tools tab and click Relationships.
Double-click the relationship line between tblOrderItem and tblProduct	To open the Edit Relationships window and create a one-to-many relationship between tblOrderItem and tblProduct.
Check the indicated options	☑ Enforce Referential Integrity ☑ Cascade Update Related Fields ☑ Cascade Delete Related Records
Click **OK**	To create the relationship.
10 Update the relationship	
Close the Relationships window	
11 Open tblOrderItem	The Product column now contains product names instead of Product ID numbers.
12 Add a new record	There are New Record buttons on the Data tab and at the bottom of the table.
Press [TAB]	To move to the Order ID cell. Order Detail ID is an AutoNumber field, and the value is assigned automatically.
Enter **27**	To specify the Order ID.

New Access features   **7–11**

13	Press (TAB)	To move to the Product cell. A dropdown arrow appears in the cell.
	Click the dropdown arrow	The list of the product names that were obtained from the tblProduct table appears, as shown in Exhibit 7-2.
	From the list, select **Chives**	To specify the product name.
14	Press (TAB)	To move to the Quantity cell.
	Enter **170**	
15	Press (TAB)	To move to the Price Paid cell.
	Enter **1.25**	
	Press (TAB)	To move to the Notes cell. The value that you entered in the Price Paid column now appears with currency formatting.
16	Update and close the table	

The attachment data type

Explanation

You can use the attachment data type to provide more detail to data in a table. Using the attachment data type, you can include documents, graphics, or other files as attachments to a field.

To use the attachment data type:

1 Open a table in Design view.
2 Add a field to house the attachment for a record.
3 Under Data Type, select Attachment.
4 Save the table.
5 Switch to Datasheet view.
6 Right-click the attachment field for the first record and choose Manage Attachments. The Attachments dialog box appears.
7 Click Add. The Choose File dialog box appears.
8 Navigate to the desired file and click Open.
9 Click OK to close the Attachments dialog box.

When you double-click the attachments field, the Attachments dialog box appears. You can then open or view the file that's attached to this record.

New Access features   **7–13**

Do it!

A-4:   Using the Attachment data type

Here's how	Here's why
1 Open tblProduct in Design view	You'll add an attachment type field to this table.
2 Select the row below strUnit	You'll insert a field.
Under Field Name, enter **productPhoto**	To specify the new field name. This field will store a photo for each product.
Under Data Type, select **Attachment**	
Under Description, enter **Thumbnail of product**	
3 Update the table	Update the table whenever you modify it.
4 Switch to Datasheet view	
5 Observe the record for **Basil Leaf (Whole)**	Basil Leaf is Product Number 28. It's the 19th record in this table. The productPhoto field displays a zero in parentheses. There are no files attached to this record.
6 Right-click the Attachment field and choose **Manage Attachments...**	To open the Attachments dialog box.
Click **Add**	The Choose File dialog box appears.
Select **bayleaf**	In the current unit folder.
Click **Open**	To select the file and close the Choose File dialog box.
7 Click **OK**	To close the Attachments dialog box. The productPhoto field now displays a 1 in parentheses.
Double-click the field	The Attachments dialog box appears.
Double-click **bayleaf**	The image displays in the computer's default viewer application.
8 Close the viewer	
Close the Attachments dialog box	
9 Update the table	

Collecting data

Explanation

If you have Outlook 2007 installed, you can use Access 2007 to create an e-mail message that includes a form that asks for specific database items. When your correspondents complete the form and reply to the e-mail, the data they send can be appended to your database or can update existing records.

To collect data by e-mail, activate the External Data tab. Click Create E-mail, and use the Collect data through e-mail messages wizard to construct the request for data and send it out in e-mail format. The first screen of the wizard is shown in Exhibit 7-3.

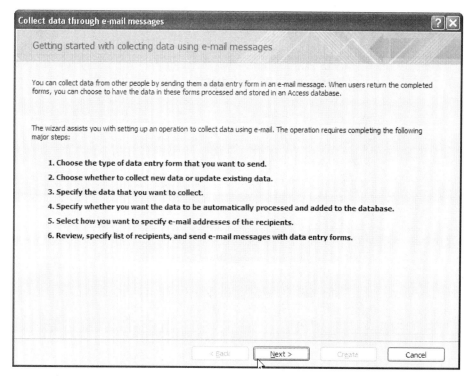

Exhibit 7-3: The first screen of the Collect data through e-mail messages wizard

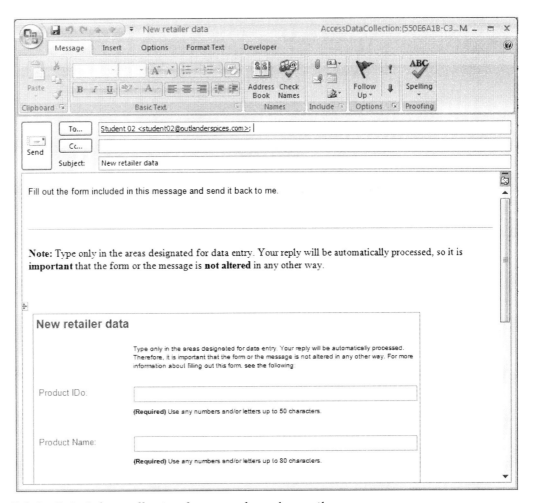

Exhibit 7-4: A data collection form sent through e-mail

Do it!

A-5: Collecting data via e-mail

Here's how	Here's why
1 Activate the External Data tab	You'll create an e-mail form that collects data.
2 In the Collect Data group, click **Create E-mail**	
	The Collect data through e-mail messages wizard appears. As shown in Exhibit 7-3, the first wizard screen describes the steps involved.
Click **Next**	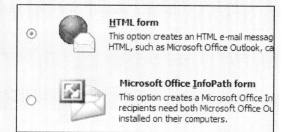
	To move to the next screen, where the type of data entry is selected. If Microsoft Office InfoPath isn't installed on this computer, then this option is disabled, and HTML form is selected by default.
3 Click **Next**	To move to the next screen, where you must choose to collect new information or update existing information.
Verify that **Collect new information only** is selected	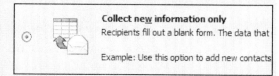
	You'll collect data to be appended to the existing database.

New Access features   **7–17**

4	Click **Next**	To move to the next screen. You'll specify the fields to be included on the form. The fields from the open table (tblProduct) appear in the Fields in table list.
	Click [>>]	To add all fields to the form.
	Observe the text in the Field Properties box	Field Properties Label to display in front of the field in the e-mail message. Unit ☐ Read-only
		This box contains a label that will display for the selected field in the e-mail message. By default, the caption entered in the database for each field is entered as the label.
5	Click **Next**	To move to the next screen, where you specify how to process replies.
	Check **Automatically process replies and add data to tblProduct**	Data will automatically be appended to the existing database when emails containing data are received.
6	Click **Next**	To move to the next screen, where you specify the email addresses of the recipients.
	Verify that **Enter the e-mail addresses in Microsoft Office Outlook** is selected	There are no e-mail addresses stored in this database.
7	Click **Next**	To move to the next screen, where you enter a subject line and body text for the e-mail message that will be sent out.
	Edit the Subject box to read **New retailer data**	Subject New retailer data
		The Introduction box explains the form to the recipient.
8	Click **Next**	To move to the wizard's last screen. This screen displays instructions on how to proceed.
9	Click **Create**	The e-mail message appears, as shown in Exhibit 7-4.
	Address the e-mail to your partner and send it	

10	Open Outlook	Choose Start, Microsoft Office, Microsoft Office Outlook 2007.
	Observe the data collection message	You should see an e-mail containing the new data collection form with the subject, "New retailer data."
	Close Outlook	
11	In Access, update and close the database	

Topic B: Reports

Explanation

Access 2007 includes a Layout view that simplifies report design. Data on reports can be sorted and grouped.

Layout view

Layout view displays a report just as it would appear on paper. While in Layout view, you can move report items and configure the report for printing. To do this, switch to Layout view, which is shown in Exhibit 7-5. Then drag and resize items on the report as desired.

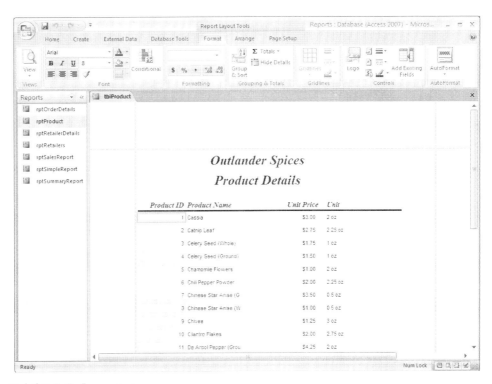

Exhibit 7-5: Layout view

7–20 Office 2007: New Features

Do it!

B-1: Using Layout view to modify reports

Here's how	Here's why
1 Open Reports	You'll use Layout view to modify the design of an existing report.
Save the database as MyReports	(If necessary.) In the Read-Only Warning, click Save As and navigate to the current unit folder.
2 Double-click **rptProduct**	(Under Reports on the Navigation pane.) The report opens in Print Preview mode.
Right-click anywhere on the report and choose **Design View**	You can use Design view to change the report, but you can't immediately see the way that changes affect the appearance of the report.
3 Right-click the report tab and choose **Layout View**	The product table report appears in Layout view as shown in Exhibit 7-5.
Close the Field List pane	If necessary.
4 Click the first number in the Product ID column	
	An orange box highlights the field to indicate that it's selected.
Point to the left side of the field	The pointer changes to a double-sided arrow.
Drag to the right	
	Reduce the field to approximately a third of its original size. The Product ID number uses a maximum of four digits, so the field doesn't have to be this large.
5 Drag the field to the right of the Unit field	
	(Point anywhere in the highlighted Product ID field, and drag to the right.) The entire column moves to the right side of the report page.
Move the column heading for the Product ID column	
	Click the column heading to select that field. Point anywhere in the field and drag to the right.
6 Deselect the field	Click anywhere on the report page.

7	Click the Product ID column heading	When you try to select the Product ID heading, the Unit heading is selected instead.
8	Activate the Arrange tab	(On the Ribbon.) You'll move the Unit column heading to the back.
9	In the Position group, click **Send to Back**	To move the Unit column heading behind the Product ID column heading.
10	Click the Product ID column heading	The field is selected now.
	Drag the field to adjust its position relative to the column	If necessary.
11	Update the report	

7–22 Office 2007: New Features

Sort and filter

Explanation

Reports in Access 2007 are more interactive than the static reports available in previous versions. A user can sort and filter records in a report just as they would in a database table or query.

To sort a report by a field, switch to Layout view. Right-click the desired field and choose Sort A to Z or choose Sort Z to A.

To filter a report, switch to Report view or Layout view. Right-click a field and choose Text Filters. Then choose a filter type. Enter the filter criteria and click OK.

Do it!

B-2: Sorting and filtering reports

Here's how	Here's why
1 Switch to Layout view	(If necessary.) You'll sort and filter this report.
2 Right-click the name **Cassia** and choose **Sort A to Z**	(From the context menu.) The report is now sorted by the Product Name field.
3 Right-click the first product name in the list and choose **Text Filters, Begins With...**	You'll filter this report to display only specific items. The Custom Filter dialog box displays.
In the strProductName begins with box, enter **cin**	**Custom Filter** strProductName begins with cin You'll display only spices that begin with these three letters. The filter isn't case-sensitive.
Click **OK**	To close the dialog box and filter the report.
4 Observe the report	Three varieties of Cinnamon are listed.
5 Resize the Product Name field to fit the product names	*Product Name* Cinnamon (Ground) Extra High Oil (2X) Click any product name to select it. Point to the right border of the field and drag to the right.
6 Switch to Print Preview	(Right-click anywhere on the report and choose Print Preview.) Print Preview shows that only the three filtered products will appear on the report if it's printed now.
7 Update and close the report	Don't close the database.
8 Open rptProduct again	Double-click the report in the Navigation pane.
Observe the report	The changes that you made to move the Product ID field and sort by Product Name are retained. The filtering by Product Name was cleared when you closed the report.

New Access features   **7–23**

9	Filter the report to display only the Cinnamon products	In Layout view, right-click a product name, and choose Text Filters, Begins With. Enter "cin" in the text box, and click OK.
10	Select a product name	If necessary.
	Right-click and choose **Clear filter from strProductName**	The filtered products display again.
11	Update and close the report	

Grouping

Explanation

You can group a report to hide report details without deleting them from the report.

To group a report:

1. Switch to Layout view.
2. On the Formatting tab, choose Grouping. The Group, Sort, and Total pane appears at the bottom of the Access window.
3. Click in the Group, Sort, and Total pane. The Group on bar appears.
4. Select the database field(s) on which to group the report.
5. If desired, click More to display more grouping options, as shown in Exhibit 7-6.

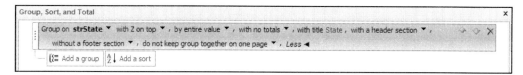

Exhibit 7-6: The Group, Sort, and Total Pane, with More grouping options displayed

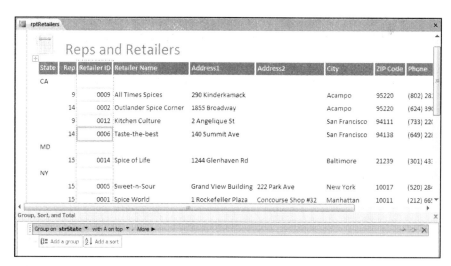

Exhibit 7-7: The report with retailers grouped by state

New Access features   **7–25**

Do it!   **B-3: Grouping report data**

Here's how	Here's why
1 Open rptRetailers	You'll use grouping to consolidate report details.
Switch to Layout view	
Activate the Format tab	If necessary.
2 Click **Group & Sort**	(In the Grouping and Totals group.) The Group, Sort, and Total pane appears below the report.
Click **Add a Group**	*Group, Sort, and Total* [≡ Add a group ↓ Add a sort]
	(In the Group, Sort, and Total pane.) The Group on bar appears. A list of database fields used in this report is superimposed over the bar.
3 Select **strState**	lngRetailerID strRetailerName strAddr1 strAddr2 strCity strState strZIPCode strFirstName strLastName strPhone strFax expression
	To group retailers by the state in which they're located.
Observe the report	The State field is now the first field on the report. Retailers have been grouped by state, as shown in Exhibit 7-7.
4 Click the arrow beside **with A on top**	**Group, Sort, and Total** Group on **strState** ▼ with A on top ▼ [≡ Add a group A↓Z Add a sort]
	To see the options for sorting the grouped report.
Select **with Z on top**	To sort the report in descending alphabetical order.

5	Observe the report	The State field is sorted in descending alphabetical order.
6	Sort the grouped report in ascending order	Click the arrow beside with Z on top, and choose with A on top.
7	Click **More**	(In the Group, Sort, and Total pane.) To see the other grouping options, as shown in Exhibit 7-6.
	Click **Less**	To hide the options.
8	Click the arrow beside **Group on strState**	You'll group the report again. The list of database fields appears.
	Select **IngRep**	(This is the last item on the list.) To group the report by the sales representatives assigned to the retailers.
9	Observe the report	The Rep field now occurs first on the report, and retailers are now grouped by Rep.
	Sort the grouping from smallest to largest	If necessary.
10	Close the Group, Sort, and Total pane	Click the Close box on the right side of the pane.
11	Update and close the report	
12	Close the database	

Unit summary: New Access features

Topic A

In this topic, you learned how to display multiple open items as **tabbed documents** instead of floating overlapping windows. Then, you created a **lookup list** using data from another table. Next, you used the **attachment data type** to attach picture files to individual records. Finally, you created an e-mail to update data.

Topic B

In this topic, you used **Layout view** to modify reports for printing. Then you used **sort**, **filter**, and **group** options to modify a report.

Independent practice activity

In this activity, you'll create a lookup list field, use the attachment data type, use Layout view to modify a report, and group the report.

1 Open PracticeReports. Save the database as **MyPracticeReports** and enable macros.

2 Open tblOrderItem in Design view.

3 Change **IngItemProductID** to a lookup list. (*Hint*: In the Data Type column, choose Lookup Wizard. Select tblProduct to provide the values.)

4 Switch to Datasheet view. Add a record, and use the lookup list to enter the Product ID. Update and close the table.

5 Open tblProduct in Design view.

6 Add a field to hold photos. Add a description. (*Hint*: Under Data Type, select Attachment.)

7 Update the table and switch to Datasheet view.

8 Add a photo for **Cloves**.

9 Update and close the table.

10 Open rptSalesReport.

11 Widen the Product column so that the column header can display, and move the column to between Order ID and Quantity. (*Hint*: Switch to Layout view.)

12 Update the report.

13 Group the report on the Product ID. (*Hint*: Display the Group, Sort, and Total pane.)

14 Close the Group, Sort, and Total pane.

15 Switch to Report view. Your report should resemble the one shown in Exhibit 7-8.

16 Update the report and close the database.

17 Exit Access.

7–28 Office 2007: New Features

rptSalesReport			
Sales Details			
Order ID	Product	Quantity	Price Paid
28	1	25	$3.00
9	1	50	$3.00
5	1	150	$3.00
27	1	200	$3.00
1	1	100	$3.00
9	2	100	$2.75
4	2	200	$2.75
25	2	50	$2.75
16	2	25	$2.75
2	3	400	$1.75
4	3	200	$1.75
22	4	80	$1.50
6	4	110	$1.50
16	4	10	$1.50
3	5	200	$1.00
300	6	20	$2.00
23	6	250	$2.00
26	6	500	$2.00
7	6	140	$2.00
26	7	400	$3.50

Exhibit 7-8: The Sales Details report after step 15 in the Independent practice activity

New Access features   **7–29**

Review questions

1 The Access 2007, tabbed documents format can be applied to legacy databases. True or false?

2 What type of field displays a list instead of a static value?

A Text field

B Lookup field

C AutoNumber field

D Attachment field

3 You can use the attachment data type to include documents, graphics, or other files as attachments to a field. True or false?

4 What's required to collect data for Access 2007?

A A Lookup wizard

B Outlook 2003

C Outlook 2007

D Microsoft Office InfoPath

5 Which view displays a report as it would appear on paper?

A Normal view

B Design view

C Page layout view

D Layout view

Course summary

This summary contains information to help you bring the course to a successful conclusion. Using this information, you'll be able to:

A Use the summary text to reinforce what you've learned in class.

B Determine the next courses in this series, if any, as well as any other resources that might help you continue to learn about Microsoft Office 2007.

S-2 Office 2007: New Features

Topic A: Course summary

Use the following summary text to reinforce what you've learned in class.

Unit summaries

Unit 1

In this unit, you used **Ribbon tabs**, **Ribbon groups**, and **galleries**. Next, you learned that **contextual Ribbon tabs** display when an item, such as a chart or diagram, is activated. You used **Live Preview** to display formatting options, and used the **Dialog Box Launcher** to open dialog boxes. You also added metadata to files by using the **Document Information Panel**. You used the Microsoft Office Button menu to open an application's Options dialog box to change default and other settings. You finished a file to make it ready to be shared with others. Next, you used the **Mini toolbar** to format content. You changed the position of the **Quick Access toolbar** and added commands to it. Finally, you used the **status bar** to change the view of a document and zoom in and out.

Unit 2

In this unit, you discussed the benefits of the **XML**-based file format used in Office 2007 files. You learned that this file format offers benefits of file size, backward **compatibility**, data **recovery**, and **extensibility**. You saved files to the previous Office format, and used the **Compatibility Checker** to find features that are not compatible with previous versions. Next, you compared **file sizes** and learned that comparable files require much less space in the Office 2007 format. You also used macro and **non-macro file formats** to allow macros or protect against security risks. Finally, you discussed the **file converters** that allow previous versions of Office applications to open Office 2007 files.

Unit 3

In this unit, you used **Styles** to format content in Word 2007, and created and formatted **charts** and basic **shapes**. Then, you used **Themes** to apply colors, fonts, and effects to an entire document. Next, you used **Quick Parts** to insert properties, fields, page numbers, or **Building Blocks** into a document. You also created custom content and save it to the Quick Parts or Building Blocks galleries. You discussed **workflows** managed by **Office SharePoint Server 2007**. You **compared multiple versions** of a document. Finally, you created **static** documents by publishing to **XPS** or **PDF** format.

Unit 4

In this unit, you discussed the changes to Excel 2007 that support **large worksheets**. Next, you created and formatted a **chart**. You created a **report** from a worksheet by using **Page Layout view**, print titles, headers, and footers. Then, you created and formatted a **table** within a worksheet, and used **structured referencing** to use names within an Excel formula. You created functions in **named tables** by using the [#This Row] argument within formulas. Next, you created and formatted **PivotTables** by using the PivotTable Field List task pane. Finally, you discussed the benefits of using **Excel Services** to share worksheets online in **HTML** format.

Course summary **S–3**

Unit 5

In this unit, you converted a bulleted list in PowerPoint 2007 to a **SmartArt graphic**. Then, you discussed sharing **slide libraries** by using Office SharePoint Server 2007. Next, you shared a presentation as a **static document** by saving it to either XPS or PDF format. Next, you discussed collaborating on presentations with **Groove 2007** or **SharePoint Server 2007**, and discussed **digital signatures**. Finally, you created **custom slide layouts**, and applied a **theme**.

Unit 6

In this unit, you used the **Instant Search** feature in Outlook 2007 to locate content in messages or other items. Then, you organized messages, appointments, tasks, and other items using **color categories**. You **previewed attachments** of Office files without opening the attachment's application. Next, you subscribed to **RSS feeds** using Outlook as an RSS aggregator. You flagged an item for follow-up, so that it would appear in the **To-Do Bar**. Then you also added tasks to the To-Do Bar. You discussed **publishing** appointment calendars online by using Microsoft Office Online. Next, you created and e-mailed a calendar **snapshot**. You created a **customized electronic business card**, and sent it via e-mail. Finally, you discussed the benefits of **Exchange Server 2007** in the areas of security, managed folders, scheduling, unified messaging, and out-of-office messages.

Unit 7

In this unit, you used the **tabbed** window display in Access 2007. Then, you created **lookup fields** for a database table, and used the **attachment** data type to attach files to a database. Then, you used Outlook 2007 to **collect** and update data automatically via e-mail. Next, you used **Layout view** to modify reports. Finally, you learned how to **sort**, **filter**, and **group** report data.

Topic B: Continued learning after class

It's impossible to learn to use any software effectively in a single day. To get the most out of this class, you should begin working with the individual Office 2007 applications to perform real tasks as soon as possible. We also offer resources for continued learning.

Next courses in this series

This is the only course in this series. We also offer a full range of courseware for all individual applications in the Office 2007 suite, including:

- *Word 2007*
- *Excel 2007*
- *Access 2007*
- *Outlook 2007*
- *PowerPoint 2007*
- *SharePoint Designer 2007*
- *Project 2007*
- *Publisher 2007*
- *Visio 2007*

Other resources

For more information, visit www.axzopress.com.

Office 2007: New Features

Quick reference

Button	Shortcut keys	Function
		Displays the Office Button menu that includes commonly used file commands, such as Open and Save As.
		Opens a dialog box, or task pane, for the corresponding ribbon group.
		Launches a gallery, or command list, from the Ribbon.
	CTRL + S	Saves, or updates, a file.
	CTRL + Z	Undoes the most recent action.
	CTRL + F6	Switches between open windows.
	CTRL + F4	Closes the open document window.
		Creates a new folder.
		Zooms in by 10% with each click.
		Zooms out by 10% with each click.
		Displays the Zoom dialog box.
		Displays the Zoom dialog box from the Ribbon.
	F1	Displays the application Help window.
		In Word, displays the document in Web Layout view.
		In Word, compares tracked changes in multiple versions of a document.

Q–2 Office 2007: New Features

Button	Shortcut keys	Function
		Adds a chart to a Word document, an Excel workbook, or a PowerPoint slide.
		Adds a chart title placeholder to the selected chart.
		Displays the Shapes gallery.
		Displays the SmartArt gallery.
		Displays the Themes gallery.
		In Excel, automatically adds a formula that calculates the total of values in the adjacent row or column.
		In Excel, displays the workbook in Page Layout view.
		In Excel, opens the Create PivotTable dialog box.
	CTRL + M	In PowerPoint, adds a new slide to the presentation.
		In Outlook, launches the Color Category dialog box.
		In Outlook, displays a list of business cards that can be inserted into a mail message.
		In Outlook, displays a list of flag options for flagging a message or other Outlook item.
		In Access, displays the selected table or report in Design view.
		In Access, starts the Collect data through e-mail messages wizard.
		In Access, displays the Group, Sort, and Total pane below the report.
		In Access, displays the Relationships window.

Glossary

Building Blocks Organizer

A library of reusable document components, such as cover pages, headers and footers, and watermarks.

Calendar snapshot

A segment of the Outlook appointments calendar that can be included as an attachment in an e-mail message. A snapshot can include one or more days and can be configured to include or exclude appointment details.

Color categories

In Outlook, a means for cataloging a message, appointment, or task by assigning it a color. The name and purpose of a color category can be customized by the user.

Compatibility Checker

A feature that searches for and lists any items in an Office 2007 file that aren't compatible—and won't be available—when the file is saved to an earlier version.

Context menu

A menu of options that displays when text or objects in a file are right-clicked.

Contextual Ribbon tabs

Ribbon tabs that display only if the file element that they control (for example, a graph) is selected.

Dialog Box Launcher

A small button in the corner of a Ribbon group that opens a dialog box with more controls.

Digital signature

A security feature that, when attached to an Office file, assures the recipient of the file creator's identity.

Document Information Panel

An area that appears below the Ribbon and contains metadata tags and other file properties.

Electronic business card

An e-mail version of a paper business card. Like a real business card, it can be customized to include contact and other information about yourself that you wish to share with others.

Excel Services

An application included in Office SharePoint Server that extends Excel functionality in an enterprise environment.

Finish

To prepare a file for sharing with others. Finishing may include inspecting the document for hidden content or personal data, restricting permission to specific users, adding a digital signature, checking for file features that aren't supported by older versions of Office, and marking the file as Final.

Gallery

A dropdown menu on the Ribbon that displays the results of each command, instead of simply the command name.

iCal

The file format used for Internet Calendars that can be published online by using Outlook.

Instant Search

An Outlook feature that's used to search for Outlook items, such as messages, contacts, appointments, meeting requests, and tasks, based on such criteria as a specific word or phrase.

Live Preview

When you point to a selection in a list or gallery, the selected text or object in the document displays the effect of that selection.

Lookup field

A type of field in Access that allows the users to select the field's entry from another table or from a list.

Metadata tags

In the Document Information Panel, items of information that describe and define the properties of a file, such as author, title, subject, keywords, category, status, and comments.

Microsoft Office Online

A Web site of tools and services published by Microsoft.

Mini toolbar

A formatting toolbar that displays when text or objects in a file are right-clicked.

Office Button

The round button displaying the Office logo that's used to display file commands for opening, saving, closing, and managing Office files.

Options dialog box

A dialog box in an Office application that contains default and customized settings for that application. The Options dialog box is launched from the File menu.

G–2   Office 2007: New Features

Phishing

An attempt to defraud by using an e-mail message that's designed to appear as though it were sent by a legitimate organization.

Quick Access toolbar

A group of frequently used commands that appears by default in the upper left of the file window, above the Ribbon. The Quick Access Toolbar can be customized to include commands and menus as needed.

Quick Parts

A gallery that provides a fast method of inserting properties, fields, and page numbers in a Word document.

Ribbon

The new Office 2007 interface feature that appears at the top of all Office windows. It's divided into tabs and groups and contains buttons, lists, and menu commands.

Ribbon groups

Sections of a Ribbon tab that may include commands, lists, menus, and galleries.

Ribbon tabs

Tabbed divisions of the Ribbon interface that display groups and individual commands.

RSS

Really Simple Syndication (RSS) is a service that delivers updates of Web content, such as news or technical topics. Outlook 2007 can act as an RSS aggregator, which receives and displays RSS feeds.

Scheduling Assistant

A feature of Microsoft Exchange Server that helps with the task of scheduling meetings for a large and geographically dispersed group.

SharePoint Server 2007

A set of enterprise-level applications designed to help users manage business content and processes. These applications reside on a server that's available to all of the users in the workflow.

Slide library

A collection of individual PowerPoint slides published to a site hosted on Office SharePoint Server. Slides in a slide library can be reused in other presentations.

SmartArt graphics

A gallery of built-in diagrams that can be used in Word, Excel, and PowerPoint to provide visual appeal.

Static document

A version of an original Office file that can't be changed after being published. Static document types include Microsoft's XPS and Adobe's PDF.

Status bar

The Status bar at the bottom of the window frame displays information about the currently open file. For Access, Excel, PowerPoint, and Word, the Status bar also contains buttons to switch the view or window, as well as controls to zoom in and out. In Outlook, the Status bar displays the number of items in the current folder.

Structured referencing

Referring to cells, ranges, or tables in Excel formulas by their names instead of by their cell addresses.

Styles

Sets of formatting options that define the appearance of recurring text components, such as headings or body text. By using a style, you can apply several formatting options in one step, and you can ensure that all similar text components have identical formatting.

Table AutoExpansion

An AutoCorrect feature. When you type in a cell adjacent to a table, Excel automatically adds it to the table and formats the top row or left column cell to match.

Theme

A formatting option that applies a complete set of formats to the entire file at once. Themes may contain colors, fonts, and effects.

To-Do Bar

Located on the right side of the Outlook window, it displays messages, appointments, and meetings that you have flagged for follow-up.

Unified messaging

A feature of Microsoft Exchange Server that can deliver voice mails and faxes to your Outlook mailbox.

Workflow

An automated set of steps that dictates what must be done to complete a file and who is to perform each step.

XML file format

The default file format for Office 2007 products. The legacy binary file format is still available but is no longer the default.

Index

A

Access
  Attachment data type, 7-12
  Collecting data, 7-14
  Document windows, 7-2
  Grouping reports in, 7-24
  Reports, 7-19
  Sorting reports, 7-22
Applications
  Galleries, 1-8
  Options, 1-5
Attachments
  Previewing, 6-8

B

Building Blocks, 3-12

C

Calendars
  Publishing, 6-17
  Snapshots, 6-18
Color categories, 6-5

D

Dialog Box Launcher, 1-15
Digital certificates, 5-10
Digital signatures, 5-10
Document Information Panel, 1-17
Documents
  Comparing versions, 3-18
  Static, 3-21, 5-7

E

Electronic business cards, 6-22
  Attaching, 6-26
Excel
  Charts, 4-3, 4-6
  Functions, 4-22
  Headers and footers, 4-12
  Page Layout view, 4-9
  PivotTables, 4-24
  Tables, 4-14, 4-20
  Worksheets, 4-2
Excel Services, 4-28
Exchange Server, 6-28
  Scheduling assistant, 6-28
  Unified Messaging, 6-28

F

Files
  Formats, 2-7
  Sizes, 2-6

I

iCal files, 6-17
Information Rights Management, 2-10
Instant Search, 6-2
Internet Calendar, 6-17

L

Layout view, 7-19
Live Preview, 1-13
Lookup fields, 7-5
Lookup lists, 7-5, 7-8

M

Macros, 2-7
Metadata tags, 1-17
Mini toolbars, 1-22
  Hiding, 1-24

O

Office Button, 1-2
Office Groove, 5-9
Options dialog box, 1-5
Outlook
  Flagging items, 6-13

P

PivotTables, 4-24
Powerpoint
  Diagrams, 5-5
PowerPoint
  Custom layouts, 5-12
  Reviewing presentations, 5-9
  Sharing presentations, 5-7
  SmartArt, 5-2
  Themes, 5-15

Q

Quick Access toolbars, 1-26
  Customizing, 1-26, 1-28
Quick Parts, 3-14
Quick Parts menu, 3-10

I–2 Office 2007: New Features

R

Really Simple Syndication (RSS), 6-10
Ribbon interface, 1-8
   Contextual tabs, 1-11
RSS feeds, 6-10

S

Shared content, 6-17
SharePoint, 5-6
SharePoint Server, 3-17
Shortcut menus, 1-22
Slide libraries, 5-6
SmartArt, 5-2
Status bars, 1-26, 1-30
Structured referencing, 4-17

T

Table AutoExpansion, 4-16

To-Do Bar, 6-13

W

Word
   Charts, 3-4
   Shapes, 3-7
   Shared documents, 3-17
   Styles, 3-2
   Themes, 3-9
Workbooks
   Sharing, 4-28
Workflows, 3-17

X

XML, 2-2
   Compatibility, 2-4

Z

Zooming, 1-30